Jameer

The Story of Jameer Nelson and How He
Came to Be a Phenomenon on the
Basketball Court and in Life

Pete Nelson
and
Elaine Whelan

www.SportsPublishingLLC.com

ISBN: 1-58261-905-0

Unless otherwise indicated, photographs are from the personal collections of Jackie and Calvin Bernard, Pete Nelson, and Fred Pickett. Every reasonable attempt has been made to determine ownership of copyright. Please notify the publisher of any erroneous credits or omissions and corrections will be made to subsequent editions.

Publishers: Peter L. Bannon and Joseph J. Bannon Sr.
Senior managing editor: Susan M. Moyer
Acquisitions editor: Dean Reinke
Developmental editor: Regina D. Sabbia
Art director: K. Jeffrey Higgerson
Dust jacket design: Kerri Baker
Project manager: Alicia Wentworth and Kathryn R. Holleman
Imaging: Kenneth J. O'Brien, Heidi Norsen, and Kerri Baker
Photo editor: Erin Linden-Levy
Vice president of sales and marketing: Kevin King
Media and promotions managers: Nick Obradovich (regional),
      Randy Fouts (national), Maurey Williamson (print)

Printed in the United States of America

Sports Publishing L.L.C.
804 North Neil Street
Champaign, IL 61820
Phone: 1-877-424-2665
Fax: 217-363-2073
Web site: www.SportsPublishingLLC.com

From a father's point of view to his son

Jameer could make any father proud of the way he
carries himself and the way he is a role model both
on and off the basketball court.

If I were to live my life over again,
I would choose to be him.

***

This book is dedicated to our grandchildren

Meer-meer (Jameer Jr.)
Boo-boo (Ruth Noelle)
(both born August 2001)
and
Bryn (Brianna Kathryn)
(born January 1995)

CONTENTS

PREFACE

For my husband Charles and me these past four years, there was nothing finer to do on a summer's evening than to grab a quick bite to eat after work and then head to Aston to see Jameer and some of the other players from our Donofrio teams play in the PureGame League. We could always count on seeing some of our friends who also loved basketball.

From the Glen Mills School, we might see their most avid and loyal fans, Ann and Al Lee. Ann had been head of food services for the boys for many years and then retired, but she and Al kept in touch, attending just about every game where the Glen Mills boys were playing. Each year as new boys came on board, they would get to know them and show they cared. The boys in turn just loved them back, almost as if they were their own grandparents. The coaches from Glen Mills, Tony, Bob and Craig, always had a team in the PureGame League and would be there to greet us and talk a little basketball.

From our Donofrio teams, we would see the Carroll brothers, Matt and Pat, and often their parents, John and Maureen, and their sister, Lauren. We had known them since they moved to our area from Pittsburgh and played with the local Hatboro-Horsham High School squad. Matt had been named Player of the Year in Pennsylvania in both his junior and senior years and had gone on to play at Notre Dame. He is now playing in the NBA with the San Antonio Spurs. For several years, as a birthday present to my husband, we would fly out to South Bend to spend a few days to see Matt play and to soak up some of the incredible spirit of Notre Dame. It was a place to be wonderfully glad to be Irish. Pat had chosen Saint Joseph's University and had the enjoyment of playing not only with Jameer but also an incredible squad over three years and of becoming well recognized for his sharp-shooting skills.

We would particularly look for the Earl Foster team that included Jameer from Saint Joseph's and Larry Yarbray from Chester High School who served as a player-coach. Here we could count on seeing some of the best basketball in the Philadelphia area. The Tri-States Sports facility where the games were held would get very hot some nights, and the players' jerseys and shorts would be totally soaked by the end of their games. And whenever Jameer was there, I could count on getting a big, sweaty hug as he greeted us after the game just as he had done since we got to know him in his high school days.

We particularly remember one evening when a player on another team who had been an All-American in college and then played in the NBA came into the warmups and made a lot of disparaging remarks about Jameer. Jameer just laughed, continued his warmups and then played his game, nailing 37 points. The regulation game ended in a tie score, and then in overtime, Jameer's final three-pointer won the game for the Earl Foster team. As always, he let his game do the talking for him.

Charles and I and sometimes our good friend, Mike Galante, would then leave, welcoming the cool evening air with lots to chat about and the goal to find a Rita's Water Ice that was still open. If that failed, there was always an all-night Dunkin Donuts with an Icy Latta somewhere along the drive home. For us, a perfect summer's night!

In the summer after his freshman year when Jameer was in Japan for the World Games helping the USA win a gold medal, we would go on the Internet before heading to Aston to print out the latest news. Since most of this was not being printed in the Philadelphia papers, we would give a copy to Pete Nelson so that he could keep up with what his son was doing and add this to his collection of news articles about Jameer's basketball games. And it was in doing this that we came to know Pete better and came to realize in the Nelson family the apple did not fall far from the tree.

Pete is very warm-hearted, very genuine in his positive outlook on life and his positive attitude toward other people. When you leave his company, you just feel that everything is all right with the world. We learned along the way that he had been the guiding force in his sons' sports activities and that whenever he could, he was there to help in whatever way he was needed. If he could not be there, he would arrange for someone else to be there for them.

He has attended just about every game Jameer has played. He liked to sit high in the stands, and when Jameer came out on the floor, he would stand up ready to give a high-five or other signal when Jameer looked up to see where he was sitting. There have been times, such as the Coaches vs. Cancer Classic held in Madison Square Garden, when Jameer ran up through the stands to give his father a big, sweaty hug and the trophy he had won.

In 2003, my book *My Mom's Making History— The Story of Computer Software, Copyrights and Creativity* was published. Its title came from an essay our daughter Christie had written when she was ten years old about our landmark U.S. Supreme Court case *Whelan v. Jaslow* that confirmed use of the copyright laws to protect computer software. After telling our own story in that book, several of our basketball friends suggested that I write Jameer's story, that his was a story worth telling. We told this to Pete after one of the PureGames the following summer, adding that it would be a better story if he told what he knew first hand about his son. He liked the idea.

That is how this book came to be. Charles and I would travel to Chester to spend an evening here and there with Pete, taping his stories, taking notes. We came to look forward to these enjoyable evenings. They were filled with lots of stories from all of us, lots of laughter and new insights, lots of things we had in common.

When the project first started, we thought this might be a self-published work produced with a small amount of money for distribution among Jameer's family and friends. Then as Saint Joseph's season became so magnificent and Jameer's leadership and athletic skills received recognition far and wide, we thought this story might be worth telling to many.

One of the insights I gained from this project was a greater understanding of how important the caring and support of a number of folks had been to Jameer's development. Sometimes people would say he had to overcome many obstacles and hardships, but that was not exactly true. Jameer had two parents who loved and truly cared about him. He did not have one good home, but two. Both were known to be great cooks and he had plenty to eat. With their subsequent marriages to other people, he had a large family of brothers and sisters and then an extended family with lots of aunts, uncles, cousins and grandparents.

His participation in sports from an early age on gave him a focus, gave him action and fun, and then later gave him the opportunity to continue his education and develop a career. Along the way, his coaches taught him not only physical skills but also the importance of teamwork and of leadership. His educators brought out in him a work ethic and confidence that he could do well with his academic studies.

What some might consider a hardship was the lack of money, but dollars were only a minor issue, an insignificant part of his life and his success. They were needed to buy better sneakers, but his sisters and others pitched in and helped. They were needed for trips and transportation, but friends and family and community groups helped with this. And then Phil Martelli came along and offered a full scholarship to college.

Academics were also a challenge for Jameer, not quite as natural as his sports, but one he took on headfirst. His parents and his educators took extra measures to assure that his grades would be good, that he would score well in his college aptitude and achievement tests, and that he would be able to handle college-level courses.

What Jameer had was a legacy of athleticism and of genuinely liking people, of appreciation and humbleness and persistence. He responded to those who cared about him and to those who were teaching him and because he did this, they took extra measures to help him. He was willing to learn and to work hard but he was also a kid who liked to have fun along the way.

When Jameer made his decision to return to college for his senior year rather than pursuing the NBA draft, we were overjoyed. We recalled telling our own son, Chad, when he was in his senior year at Gettysburg College to cherish this time. Never again would he have such easy access to friends and to learning experiences. One day in the not too distant future, he would have a job and work responsibilities and then likely family responsibilities. Friends to just relax and share your life with would be less available as they, too, would become involved in work and family.

When Jameer told his teammates his decision to stay at Saint Joseph's, they all surprised him and gave him hugs, something they had never done before. Jameer said he just wanted to be a kid for one more year and to have fun working with his teammates to have a winning season. We were glad for him, that he would have this special time before facing, as he put it, the real world. Little did we realize just how special it would be.

What set him apart, we think, were not just his athletic skills but also his heart and his spirit. I recall when he returned from Japan sporting a new tattoo, he explained its meaning to me and made me realize each one had a deep spiritual meaning to him.

Among my own mentors, helping me to be the best I could be, were Miriam and Herbert Frank. When I was young, they taught me a little verse that became part of me. I do not know its origin, but because they were Quakers, I think the verse might also be. It goes: "They drew a circle and shut me out, heretic, rebel, a thing to flout. But love and I had wit to win, we drew a circle and took them in."

This is what Jameer does—he draws a circle and takes people in. It is his own special brand of leadership, not necessarily with physical hugs, but hugs nonetheless to help others be all they can be.

As the years go by, I will remember his amazing plays, but I think what I will remember most about Jameer is his holding little Meer-meer in his arms, his smiling eyes and face and those big, wonderful, sweaty hugs.

—Elaine Whelan

Acknowledgments

First and foremost, we would like to thank...

Christie Hartmann for her expert editing of this book.

Robert Hartshorn for his inside look at the wonderful collection of players that made up the St. Joseph's basketball team.

Phil Martelli for his insights and review of the years coaching Jameer at Saint Joseph's University.

Fred Pickett for his recollections and stories from the years he coached Jameer at Chester High School and for his eloquence and commitment to the city of Chester.

Charles "Chuck" Whelan for his participation in the driving, story-telling, confirmation of sports facts, first editing and all-around support for this project.

We would also like to thank those who contributed their stories and recollections and helped us with our research...

Jackie and Calvin Bernard
Tyona Burton
Robert "Nas" Clark
Pat Doherty

Mike Galante
Keddy Harris
Elijah Holmes, Sr.
Randy Legette
Stephen Michael Lewis
Rob Knox
Tom Konchalski
Elsie Plummer Nelson
Walt "Ozz" Ostrowski
Wanda Pickett
Monte Ross
Jeremy Treatman
Dick Vitale
Jerry Wainwright
Dick Weiss
Gene Whelan
Jay Wright

—Elaine Whelan and Pete Nelson

I would like to pay great tribute to all of Jameer's coaches. Here, to the best of my memory, are their names:

T-Ball	Ted Ott
Football	Ed Long
	Vince Long
	Rich Lubicki
	Newt
	Morgan
	Bill Miller
	Bill Hudson
Baseball	Calvin Bernard
	(and Pete Nelson!)
Basketball	Joe Griffith
	Clara Johnson
	John Shelton, Jr.
	Fred Pickett
	Keddy Harris
	Fred Moon
	Derrick Spence
	Keith Taylor
	Terry Thomas
	Larry Yarbray
	Phil Martelli
	Mark Bass
	Matt Brady
	Monte Ross

—Pete Nelson

INTRODUCTION

In the basketball season of 2003-2004, there was magic in the air throughout the Philadelphia area.

Jameer Nelson had made his decision to return to Saint Joseph's University to complete his senior year after attending the NBA pre-draft camp and giving serious consideration to entering the NBA draft. He said he wanted to be a kid for one more year and have fun being with his teammates, working together for a winning season.

After mounting success after success in his first three years playing college ball and dazzling many with his movements and leadership on the court, there were high hopes that this would not only be a winning season for St. Joe's but also that individual and team records could reach new heights.

Tried and true sports fans know from experience that many things can go wrong…there can be injuries, sicknesses and dissension among players, conflicts with the coach, sometimes just bad luck and always the possibility of competitors who are stronger and more formidable. But confidence in the positive possibilities prevailed. It was going to be a very good year.

By the end of their storybook season, Jameer became the most celebrated athlete not only at Saint Joseph's University, but also in the history of the National Collegiate Athletic Association. He was honored not only for his athletic skills but also for the leadership, unselfishness, humanity and team spirit he brought to collegiate sports. How did he become this person?

Perhaps you will gain greater insight, perhaps some of your curiosity will be satisfied, as his father Pete Nelson and friend Elaine Whelan tell his story beginning at birth through his early school days and then his years playing basketball in high school and college and preparing for a professional career.

CHAPTER 1

The Story Begins

South of Philadelphia, Pennsylvania, along the Delaware River and its shipyards is the city of Chester. This is where Jameer Nelson was born on the ninth of February in 1982, the third child of Linda and Floyd "Pete" Nelson. It was the shipyards and a job as a welder that drew his father to Chester after his service in the Marine Corps during the Vietnam War.

Jameer had two older brothers, one also called Pete and another named Jabre. Jabre was born with a defective heart and survived only three months. His oldest brother, Pete, had his father's sturdy build and followed his love of sports, concentrating on football but also playing basketball.

Although a child was supposed to be five to play with the local Brookhaven Jets football team,

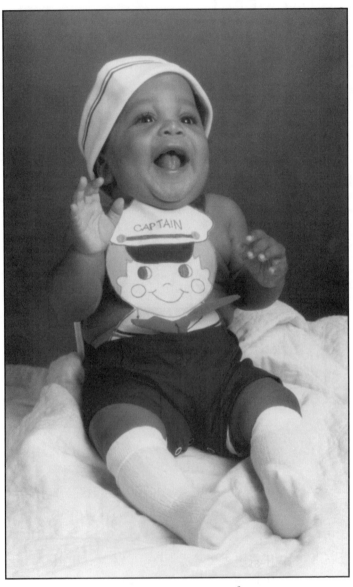

Jameer at six months.

it was no surprise when his father signed Jameer up at four and waived the insurance so that he could play. Then the following Christmas, there was an indoor basketball court under the tree. Starting with his preschool days at the Thomas Learning Center and then through his years at Toby Farms Elementary in Chester Township, Jameer started shooting baskets every day after school.

In these early years, Jameer was a three-sport guy. Also beginning at the age of five, Jameer participated in t-ball and baseball. He proved to be so talented that his coaches moved him up to the pee-wees as a pitcher and second baseman. His father had played baseball and thought then that this would become Jameer's number-one sport.

Those who knew him then said that he was the happiest kid. Even as a baby, Jameer seldom cried. He was, however, persistent in letting everyone know when he wanted something. His life centered around school, sports and his family. Although his parents divorced, they lived near each other, stayed friends with one another, and Jameer essentially lived with both of them.

In addition to his big brother Pete, nearby were his half-sisters Tamira and Althea and later a younger half-brother, Maurice. All were close and continued to be close and supportive throughout the years. Tamira was the least interested in sports

Jameer at age eight with sister Althea, uncle James Holland Jr., and niece Brianna.

but excelled in school. Althea focused on softball and proved to be a champion. Maurice is ten years younger than Jameer and has concentrated on basketball, also playing point guard and showing great promise.

Now it seems that no matter how fine sounding your name is, others will give you a nickname. If your name is short, it will be lengthened. If it is long, it will be shortened. Or folks will come up with still something else. From when he was a little baby, Jameer's parents called him "Booby" and soon everyone in his family and many others in the Toby Farms neighborhood were also calling him this. This name stuck until he turned ten or eleven, and then he became "Jameer" again, the name chosen by his godmother, Fran Tinnell. Years later, when he was playing basketball for Saint Joseph's University, his old friend Shnika Bernard called out "Hey, Booby" from the stands. Somehow Jameer heard his old nickname and looked up to see just who might be calling out to him.

The family was well known in Chester, not only for their children's activities, but also due to father Pete's reputation at the barbeque pit. He had learned to barbeque from his father-in-law, James Holland, and developed his own secret recipe for the sauce. He cooked his special ribs, chicken and ground sirloin on a big outdoor pit and became renowned in the Chester area. It was a special treat for family and friends to be invited to one of the Nelson family barbeque picnics.

Because there were not many organized activities for young children in their neighborhoods, Pete and other fathers cut back on their own sports in their mid-thirties and instead joined forces to organize and coach baseball, basketball and football teams for their children.

DIDJA HEAR 'BOUT JAMEER?

WHEN I FIRST MET *Pete and Linda, our daughter Shnika was just one and our son Calvin was three months old. While I worked, Linda would care for our children. Then their son Jameer was born. Since he was a little baby, he always liked balls. When he could walk, he would be bouncing a ball between his legs and around his back.*

My husband, Calvin, and Pete were the best of friends. Through their friendship, the boys too became the best of friends. Even though our son Calvin was older, they seemed like they were the same age. The boys started playing t-ball when Jameer was about four.

Every Saturday morning, Jameer would come over as soon as daylight broke, wanting to play. Jameer and Calvin collected baseball cards and spent a lot of time playing and talking about sports. At first it was mostly football and baseball, but then in high school Jameer made the decision to go with basketball. Calvin is now a senior at Cheyney University, still loves sports and would love to be a sports commentator. Shnika is close to Jameer, still loves to call him Booby and refuses to give it up.

—Jacqueline "Jackie" Bernard,
Longtime family friend

Jameer, age 13, with Maurice,
age three.

CHAPTER 2

Growing Up in Chester

One of the remarkable things about Jameer during his years growing up in what is known as a tough town has been that no one can remember him ever getting into a fight.

There is one story, however, in which he came darn close. He had won a superb Mongoose bike playing baseball, that had become his pride and joy. It was an expensive bike with lots of cool features, but one day along came an older boy who tried to mess with it. Jameer asked him to leave the bike alone, but he would not stop. Using all his strength, Jameer simply picked up the older, much larger fellow and flipped him to the ground, a move that is known in professional wrestling as a body slam. Word spread throughout the town and

Jameer, age seven, at Pete's house.

from that day forward, no one in Chester picked on Jameer Nelson again.

When Jameer was 11 or 12, one of his friends, Elijah Holmes, was injured in an automobile accident when traveling with his grandmother. Elijah suffered a broken neck in three places and his teammates were told that he would not be playing basketball for a long time. Jameer asked his coach if, to honor Elijah and show his support, he could wear his No.15 jersey until Elijah recovered. The coach said yes, and when Jameer came out running for the next game, he had on Elijah's shirt. Elijah's father recalled that not only he, but also many of the other parents, were taken by surprise and had tears in their eyes. Until the day Elijah recovered and could return to the court, Jameer wore No. 15.

One day when Elijah's father, also named Elijah, was talking with Jameer and his father, he handed a piece of paper to Jameer who was nearby doing his homework. Elijah said to him, "Here, practice signing your name, because someday people are going to be asking you for your autograph." Jameer laughed, but remarkably, Elijah Sr.'s words came true about ten years later.

Jameer signs autographs after a Saint Joseph's team practice. (AP/WWP)

DIDJA HEAR 'BOUT JAMEER?

I BECAME FRIENDS with Jameer and his father when my son Elijah Jr. played sports with Jameer in Chester Township and have now been friends with them for over 17 years.

From when he was about six, Jameer was a man among boys. He would come down court, stop, put the ball between his legs and get the ball to where it was supposed to be. When he was nine, he ran 33 touchdowns in one season and took his team to the championship. I was so sure of his talent that one day when I was at their house watching a basketball game with his dad, I told Jameer to start practicing signing his name, that one day he would be signing a lot of autographs. He looked at me like I was crazy and laughed, but started writing his name. After about ten of them, he said: "Can I stop now?"

People can say I'm crazy, but I'm usually right about these things. In every sport he played, Jameer would get MVP. Sometimes, the parents of other boys would be jealous and tell us their kids didn't stand a chance.

Jameer had a lot of support from both of his parents. Pete would often get up and out the door very early in the morning to transport the boys to games. All that is happening now is happening to the right people. The Nelsons are the best, and I will never forget them.

—Elijah Holmes Sr.
family friend

Jameer, age 10, with MVP and Chester Biddy League championship trophies

Pete met first Calvin Bernard when his wife, Linda, was helping to care for the two Bernard children, Shnika and Calvin III. They became the best of friends and played on local softball teams together until they were in their mid-30. When Calvin III and Jameer were old enough, they would come out to see their fathers play. Both fathers recalled that when Jameer was five and Calvin III was seven, they got into a fight and were crying. Both boys got a talking-to by their dads, made up and thereafter were the best of friends.

The young Calvin, like Jameer, was a natural at sports. The boys would find new games to play. One called "rundown" was a version of baseball that could be played in their driveway. Both excelled at football, and the older Calvin thought this would become Jameer's sport. He also coached Jameer in Little League baseball and would get together with Pete to take the boys to the Phillies games. When Medford Franks started including coupons in their hot dog packages for free admission to the Phillies, they included more young boys and piled them all into both of their cars to drive to the game.

Jameer with Crozer Chargers football MVP trophy.

DIDJA HEAR 'BOUT JAMEER?

I ALWAYS THOUGHT that Jameer was more of a football player. I have fond memories from when he played in the Crozer League. He was a natural, very graceful athlete who could have played any sport. In one football game, he scored six touchdowns. When he was injured, you would think there was no way he would be able to return to the game, but somehow he did.

Over the years, no matter what sport he was playing, he had the skills and unorthodox moves and all eyes would tend to focus on him. In football, he was the fastest quarterback and fastest running back that his dad and I ever saw. In one funny incident, Jameer moved left, then right so adeptly that he faked another player right out of his shoes. His dad also had unorthodox moves when he played sports.

Jameer was always ahead of schedule. When he was five or six he could make 10-foot baskets at an age when most of the other kids could not. When Jameer was at the Main Street Middle School, they would go to great lengths to track him down after school so they could bring him over to the high school to play.

Throughout high school and college, I came to just about every one of his games, often traveling with Pete in his old red Sanford & Son truck. I think Phil Martelli brought out the man in Jameer in a controlled way. Although Jameer could have showboated, he chose not to.

—Calvin Bernard Jr.,
family friend and former coach

1992 Toby Farms Baseball, AA MVP team. Jameer is center, front row, holding baby Maurice with coach Pete Nelson on right of back row and coach Calvin Bernard on left of back row.

Once they obtained special permission to bring the boys into the left field of the Vet (Philadelphia's Veteran Stadium). Full of fun, the boys started to pretend they were in a real game, bouncing off the left field wall to catch high-flying balls. For many games, they would try to get there early enough to see batting practice and, if lucky, get a ball. Each boy was told he could have one hot dog and one drink and that was all. The boys would bring along their gloves and baseballs to wait for autographs from the Phillies players afterward and, if there were fireworks, stay late into the night.

After their own games, Pete Nelson would take the whole team somewhere for a treat. He recalls that Jameer would want a banana boat at the Dairy Queen. Pete would say no, he could only have whatever they could afford to buy for the whole team. Jameer would insistently say, "But you're my father," and Pete would be equally insistent in saying no, it was not the right thing to do. After a few rounds of this, Jameer agreed that his father was right, but said that when it was just the two of them out together, he wanted his banana boat.

Known only to father and son for quite a few years, Pete thought this story would be their secret forever: After his parents divorced, Jameer was told by his mother that he would not be allowed

Jameer and his mom, Linda.

to play sports for a while as punishment for getting a bad mark in his school work. Pete came by and told Linda that he wanted to take Jameer out just for ice cream and she agreed. Instead, Pete secreted Jameer off to play basketball in Chester's Biddy League. Many years later, when being interviewed his junior year in college by the *Philadelphia Inquirer* for a newspaper article, Jameer gave away their long-held secret.

Still another family story is this one: When he was seven years old, Jameer hit his first homerun in baseball. As it was a tradition to be awarded

Jameer at age seven (far left) in Chester Biddy League, third from left is Ramee Davis.

your home run ball, Jameer wanted to save his, but as hard as everyone tried, it could not be found. His father plucked a new ball out of the pile in the dugout, walked away from the game and hit it against a tree a number of times to make it look worn. He came back to the game and presented this to Jameer so that he could have a treasured ball.

Once when Jameer was pitching, there was a player on third edging forward like he was going to steal home and score a run. From his mound,

Jameer looked to the home plate and faked a throw to the catcher and in one swift motion, ran to third and tagged the kid out. The coaches there say that to this day, they have never seen a move quite like Jameer's.

Not a true nephew, but called a nephew by Jameer's father, was a family friend Robert Clark, better known as "Nas." Pete would ask Nas to look out for Jameer when he could not and when the young people were out together. Not having a father at home, Nas was drawn to the Nelson family and looked to Pete as his father figure. He was like a big protective brother to Jameer, and they became very close. They would hang out, talk about life, and challenge each other at video games and basketball. Nas tells the story of how he once beat Jameer at the baskets, but the little kid on the next round did him in, 11 to 0.

Knowing Jameer would take the challenge and want to prove them wrong, he would "work from negativity" and tell Jameer some of the critical things being said about him around town. The next thing he knew, Jameer would be working his heart out to improve whatever they said was wrong about him or his game. Having seen other teenagers resort to selling drugs to earn money and wanting Jameer never to even consider doing this, he would volunteer to give some of his hard-

DIDJA HEAR 'BOUT JAMEER?

JAMEER IS A COMPETITOR. He has fire in him. In the beginning when he was playing basketball, people would say he couldn't shoot, that he was too short, that he had no jumper. I would tell him these negatives and the next thing I knew, he would be at work to overcome whatever bad was said about him. We would work out and lift weights together, play video games and shoot baskets. We spent a lot of time just hanging out and talking and I can tell you he's a joker.

Although he has learned to speak in front of groups, he was basically shy and not comfortable with this to start. When he started to get tattoos, they were meant to speak for him, to express what he was thinking. Now, his son is a reflection of him. He adores him and tries to be with him whenever possible.

When he was struggling with his decision on whether to leave college after his junior year to join the NBA draft, I told him to come back, that he could break records and that his No. 14 jersey would be retired. But I did not imagine all that could happen his senior year. One night recently, Jameer called and we were supposed to meet at eight, but he was signing autographs. Finally, after 10 he called and said he'd signed so many autographs, he had to go home and take a shower.

He's become like a little brother to me. I think he has the heart of a lion and I am very happy to have had a hand in his development.

—Robert "Nas" Clark,
family friend

Robert "Nas" Clark, Jameer, and Pete in
Buffalo, New York, 2004 NCAA
Tournament.

earned dollars whenever he thought they might be needed.

Although Chester is known as a tough town, it is also a great sports town and has produced many outstanding athletes. On the playing fields and basketball courts, competition was always strong and relentless. From the city kids, Jameer would hear that he was not so great because he came from Toby Farms out in Chester Township. And his typical reaction? He laughed...and kept on playing, kept on improving, kept on building his confidence.

As he grew into his teenage years, what Jameer wanted was a really good pair of sneakers. But the best ones cost $75, and no one had $75. His sisters and others among his family and friends voluntarily added the dollars he needed and, as a group project, the sneakers were bought.

Because of his ship-building skills and experience, Pete received offers for good jobs in other cities when his children were growing up. He always turned them down because he wanted to be home for his kids and to be able to watch them play their sports and give them a guiding hand whenever it was needed.

CHAPTER 3

Basketball Becomes His Sport

Throughout elementary and junior high school, Jameer continued to play all three sports—baseball, basketball and football. When he was in eighth grade, he was moved up to the Chester High School varsity baseball team. This same year, he played on the high school's junior varsity football and basketball teams.

Each of his coaches would become upset because of his participation in the other sports. Those who wanted him to play baseball or football would say he was far too short to do well in basketball. Although in earlier times, playing a number of sports and being a "three-letter man" was considered a great thing, many thought that it was best to concentrate on just one. In a number of sports that had previously been identified with

Jameer, age nine, playing indoor basketball.

one season, year-round activities such as camps, games, and tournaments developed along with the need for greater commitment on the part of the players.

During the summers, Jameer would play baseball during the day and then head off to Smedley Junior High School to continue with basketball into the evening hours. In the fall, he would play football and, with his strong, accurate arm, was very successful as a quarterback. Encouraged by his stepmother, Elsie, who thought it to be too rough a sport, football was the first of the three sports he gave up.

When he was in eighth grade and playing on the high school JV basketball team, Fred Pickett was the varsity coach. Fred and his wife, Wanda, had known Jameer since his preschool days when he played with their son Shawn at Concord Day Care Center. Wanda often talked to her husband about how good Jameer was at sports even as a very small youngster. Both remembered how he often had a big smile on his face and was just simply happy. Fred first asked Jameer if he wanted to come along with the older boys to a basketball camp. He remembers that Jameer was kind of shy and not sure of himself, but said yes. Fred next asked Pete if his son could come, and he too said yes.

So along with the rest of the team, Fred and Jameer traveled to a summer basketball camp at Alvernia College, a small Catholic college in Reading, Pennsylvania. Jack McCluskey, the Alvernia coach, arranged for the boys to stay overnight in the dormitories and get a first taste of college life.

It was in these camp days that Jameer started to think that he might go to college one day and another special story came to be. Fred remembers that one of the college coaches said about Jameer: "Fred, that kid is going to be good. Is he a junior?" Another one of the college coaches watched Jameer play at Alvernia and said, "I want him on

DIDJA HEAR 'BOUT JAMEER?

I FIRST NOTICED JAMEER when he was about seven or eight, before I met and married his father. I was at BP's Family Day in Clemonton Park, New Jersey, with my nieces and nephews. Jameer did not want to ride the train that goes around the park, but instead headed to the basketball courts.

Later, when I became part of his family, I was working two jobs but was always

Jameer with Elsie and Pete at BP Family Day in Trainer, Pennsylvania.

Jameer with cotton candy and Pete at
BP Family Day.

*trying to get a written game schedule so that
I could plan to attend as many of his games
as possible.*

*When Pete, Jameer and I were out for
a family day at Hershey Park, I recall
Jameer playing one of the games where you
had to pay a dollar and make baskets to
win a ball. After he won six balls, the deal-
er said he couldn't take his dollar any more.
The other kids said: "Here's my dollar, shoot
for me." Jameer went on to win eight more
balls and gave them all to the kids around
him.*

—Elsie Plummer Nelson,
wife to Pete, stepmother to Jameer

our team next year"...to which Fred Pickett said, "Do you know he is just coming out of eighth grade?"

When Jameer was in eighth grade and playing on the high school varsity baseball team, Fred had a conversation with Jameer's father, Pete, about how good Jameer had been at basketball. At that time, Pete thought that baseball was Jameer's best sport. Fred pointed out that they were living in a basketball town and this might be the best athletic avenue for Jameer. But the one who made the decision was Jameer. Somehow at this age, the basketball bug bit him, and he decided he wanted to play.

As a ninth grader, the high school coaches allowed Jameer to play with them in the off season, but when they discussed it in their coaches meetings, they determined that at this age a boy might be physically ready for varsity sports but not mentally.

And so it was that when it came to playing high school varsity basketball, Jameer would wait until his sophomore year. In his very first game, a big sellout against powerhouse Harrisburg High School, the score was nip and tuck all the way. Jameer had played well and appeared to be taking the game over. Then he experienced cramps, played more and then had cramps again and had to be taken out of the game. Harrisburg won by a small margin, but the consensus was that if Jameer could have stayed in, it might have been Chester's victory.

During his years at Chester High School, Jameer continued to hone his basketball skills. He was unselfish in giving the ball to his older teammates, among them Andre Morton, Kenny Tate and Ramee Davis. He was said to "deliver the mail," and "nobody quite gave the ball like he did" and came to be loved and appreciated by the older guys on the team. As he had done since he was five, he was playing ahead of his age. A new nickname, "Young 'Un," was bestowed upon him by the coaches and players.

Jameer was taught to be the "terminator." This is a revered position that was considered by many aficionados the most dreaded high school basketball defense in the PIAA (Pennsylvania Interscholastic Athletic Association). It was originally given its name by coach Alonzo Lewis, Fred's predecessor at the school. In this position, Chester was able to use Jameer's earlier skills as a quarterback in football to further improve its own exceptional defenses. The person assigned to be the terminator must orchestrate the movement of players and cover a good portion of the court as he makes quick and rational decisions to plug up any holes that may come from the opposing offensive team. The sideline and baseline players will contribute to the controlled press, but it is the terminator who makes the adjustments. As Fred has said:

DIDJA HEAR 'BOUT JAMEER?

THE DAY I KNEW JAMEER *was a special player was as a sophomore.*

We went to Harrisburg to play the Cougars, who the previous year had beaten us soundly in the state playoffs. They had their whole team returning. We had Kenny Tate, Ramee Davis and a few role players back. We started horribly and were down by ten points when this sophomore point guard, in his second or third varsity game, stepped up and led his team from behind. We led most of the game until he started to cramp up with four minutes remaining. Harrisburg came back to win by three points. But this game left an indelible mark across the state of Pennsylvania about this sophomore from Chester. Harrisburg went on to win the PIAA AAAA state title that year.

But that game helped establish the legend that is Jameer Nelson.

—Kedrick "Keddy" Harris,
Assistant basketball coach,
Chester High School

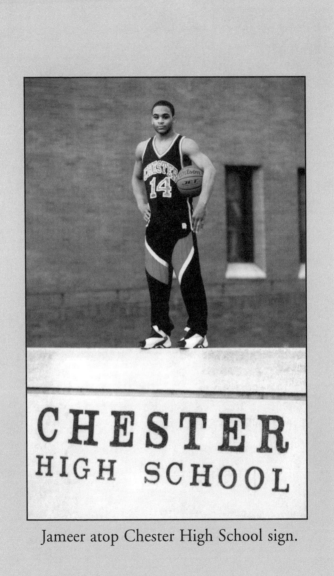

Jameer atop Chester High School sign.

Jameer, age 19, with Ernest Pearsall of
Youth Interlock Society.

"Sometimes it looks like we run around like crazy out there on the floor, but there is a method to what we are doing." And it has been a method that has helped to make the Chester High basketball program a major success.

Dr. Earl Pearsall, a Chester native who was active in sports activities for young people, noticed Jameer and took a special interest in him. He arranged for his son, Ernest Pearsall, to help Jameer with his academics and before long, Jameer moved up from being a C- student to a solid B average. As the prospect of heading to college became very real, the Pearsalls continued to provide academic counseling whenever Jameer needed it and arranged for extra tutoring to help him

Coach Fred Pickett with assistants Larry Yarbray and Derrick Spence (right).

prepare for his SAT (Scholastic Achievement Testing) exams.

Jameer's teachers at Chester High also provided extra measures to help him, citing that he was very likeable, humble and honest, never a problem child. He was also very well liked by his classmates and could often be seen helping them with their schoolwork.

His coach, Fred Pickett, proved to be a strong influence in Jameer's decision to concentrate on basketball rather than his other sports. Coached by Fred along with his assistants, Larry Yarbray, Keddy Harris, Derrick Spence, Fred Moon, Terry Thomas and Keith Taylor, Jameer continued to improve each year and to take on the role of team leader.

Assistant coach Larry Yarbray had been an outstanding point guard at Coppin State and helped them win a spot in the NCAA Tournament. After he completed college, Fred had tried to recruit him to help with the Chester High team, but at first Larry was reluctant, still wanting to be involved in playing himself. When Jameer joined the high school squad, Larry agreed to come on board and was given the special assignment of guiding Jameer to become the best point guard he could be. During the off season, Larry also coached him in the Youth Interlock Society that was formed as Jameer was entering his senior year. They formed a strong friendship that continued through Jameer's college days when Larry was player-coach and Jameer a player on the Earl Foster team in the summer PureGame league.

All of the assistant coaches at Chester High were recruited from former players on the team. Derrick Spence played the terminator position of the Clippers press in 1989 when they played Glen Mills five times in the same year and won the PIAA state championship. Fred Moon, also an ex-Clipper and a player for Duquesne University, was the freshman coach before becoming an administrator, but he still volunteered to help out with the team.

Keith Taylor had also been a point guard for the Clippers and had played at Central State before joining the coaching staff in charge of the junior varsity squad. He often sat down with Jameer and had many conversations with him about running the ball club and what it meant to be a Clipper and wear the orange and black uniform. Keith was able to troubleshoot wherever it was needed on both teams. Keddy Harris was an unpaid but very enthusiastic and talented volunteer whose goal was to make everyone the best they could be.

When Jameer first came on board with the varsity team, they already had an outstanding point guard in Naeem Scott, so he was asked to play the No. 2 guard position. Jameer was told he had to nourish Naeem early in the game, then in the last quarter, they would switch with Naeem taking the No. 2 spot and Jameer going to the point. Although Jameer initially held back his offensive skills, he began to re-create himself during his sophomore season.

The following summer, others thought his skills were good enough to get an invitation to the prestigious ABCD camp held at Fairleigh Dickinson University in New Jersey each year for the most outstanding high school players in the nation. Jameer was not a shoo-in for the camp. Telephone calls were made by Fred, Earl Pearsall, Bill Ellerbee and Sam Rines on his behalf and an invitation arrived. There were three outstanding

DIDJA HEAR 'BOUT JAMEER?

IN JAMEER'S JUNIOR YEAR, we had come back to Chester after we played a game. I was not in my house 30 minutes when the phone rang and it was Jameer. My first thought was that he must have forgotten something on the bus. But what he wanted from me was to go the Chester Boys Club to work on some of his ball-handling skills.

We didn't talk much on the way about just what he wanted to do. I noticed after watching him a while that everything he was doing was with his left hand—dribbling, shooting, going behind his back—and realized this must be where he felt he needed work.

I can tell you Jameer is special not only because he is talented, but also because he is willing to work hard. This has become his trademark, his wanting to work hard.

In Jameer's senior year, I was having a conversation with the coach trying to decide whether to reserve rooms for the next level of the Eastern Finals. If we didn't win the *next game, the school would be out $275 for the room deposits. Jameer happened to walk in on this conversation and simply said: "Order the rooms—we'll be there." I did and at the next standing-room-only game at Villanova, we won. After that game, NBA player Richard Hamilton came over to talk to Keddy Harris and motioned to Jameer. He said: "Keep working hard, kid. You'll be in the league someday."*

Each year at Chester, Jameer took on more of the responsibility, more of the leadership for the team. He was low key in getting it done in a nice, quiet, respectful way. I remember him saying to the others: "Fellas, remember how hurt we were two weeks ago when we lost by one. Well, we're not going to let that happen tonight."

And they didn't.

—Randy Legette,
Athletic director and former player,
Chester High School

Jameer (in a Chester High School game against Williamsport) worked hard on his ball handling.

point guards at the camp that year, among them Omar Cook. These players were assigned to the best teams, Jameer to a mediocre team. His playing skills and his ability to "run the team" caught the eye of several college coaches. Similar phrases, such as "This Jameer kid is good"…"This Jameer kid is very talented"…"This Jameer kid is something else" began repeating. Jameer's stock was rising with each game, and when he came back home, he knew he belonged out there with the best.

Jameer always studied the game, taking note of how the outstanding players did their jobs. In his junior year, another point guard, Jason Williams, who played at St. Joseph's High in New Jersey and went on to play at Duke, was considered the best in America. Jameer was told that he possessed a lot of the same qualities, and this was another step toward building his confidence, reinforcing the idea that he should strive to be the best he could be. From the start Jameer bought into the concept that it takes five guys, and everyone has to play their part.

During the district playoffs at Norristown High School, Jameer was sitting in the stands when Marques Green, the outstanding point guard from Norristown High, came up to him. Marques was overheard by several guys saying to Jameer: "There's only one suburban player good

enough to play Division I ball…and you're looking at him!" Jameer just looked up at him and
grinned. It's unclear whether this was just a little
woofing—what is known as basketball trash
talk—or whether Marques was serious. At that
time, some of the basketball analysts thought
Marques was the better point guard, others gave
their nod to Jameer. Marques went on to a stellar
career at St. Bonaventure, played against Jameer in
the Atlantic 10 conference and let it be known
publicly that he, too, admired Jameer Nelson.

Later, at the Prime Time Shootout at the
Sovereign Bank Arena in New Jersey, Jameer met
up with Omar Cook again as a senior and defend-
ed well, stripping him several times. At the end of
the game, the exhausted Omar said as he was
shaking hands with the players and coaches from
Chester: "This might have been the toughest
game I ever played."

When the Chester Clippers played against
Red Bank in New Jersey, they were up against several players headed to Division I ball in college
and all were up there at 6'7", 6'8", 6'9" and were
able to beat them. This further solidified the confidence and cohesion of the Chester team.

In Jameer's senior year when Chester was
playing against Hatboro-Horsham in the playoffs,
he came down with a serious case of the flu. When
the coaches had gathered everyone for the pregame talk, they noticed Jameer was not there.

Coach Harris reported that he was in the bathroom and having a very hard time. Jameer came out for the warmups but then had to leave again during the National Anthem. Fred told him he was too sick to play, but Jameer said: "You gotta let me play, Coach." Fred saw the intense look in his eyes and said he would let him start, but if it did not go well, he would have to take him out.

Chester had a great trainer in Ken Santello, who went to work on Jameer every chance he could get to bring down the fever and keep his body cool. Chester was way behind at the start, but Jameer seemed to forget he was sick and played the whole game so intently, with extraordinary determination and focus, that they ended up winning. After the end of their victorious game, he went back to being sick, but he said it was a "happy sick."

The buildup of player skills and cohesion culminated in a truly outstanding team by Jameer's senior year. Their coach said about them: "This team is very focused. They have a great resiliency about them. They know what to do. And they don't just listen, they do what they're told." Game by game, the Chester High Clippers led by Jameer, Yankuba Camara, Naeem Scott, Ray Strickland, Lateef Watts and the rest of the team, defeated their competitors and then moved through the playoffs to become the 2000 Pennsylvania PIAA Class AAAA State Champions.

DIDJA HEAR 'BOUT JAMEER?

WHEN JAMEER WAS *playing for Chester High School, we would meet them not only in regular-season play but also in district playoffs. I recall that every time they needed a big shot, a big play, Jameer was right there for them. He never got flustered.*

You would think you had him figured out, but you didn't. He is very crafty. We could never win against him, and to this day, we have not won against Chester.

The only place I have gone to more games than our own has been St. Joseph's. When Pat Carroll from our team joined the squad, I was there mainly to see him, but then also got the benefit of seeing Delonte West and Jameer develop. I thoroughly enjoyed being there. It was just a pleasure to watch the way St. Joe's played.

When he missed that last shot against Oklahoma State in the Elite Eight, what went through my mind was that he would have made it if the uniforms were black and red. He took the very same shot against us a number of times, he took it at Norristown in the district playoffs, and he made it every time.

I had enjoyed seeing Jameer play in Conshohocken, when he was on Chuck Whelan's team for the Donofrio Classic. I noticed that he got a lot of good advice and took it. No one at that time expected quite what has happened with Jameer. He has grown into a responsible man with a family. He has been smart enough to keep good people around him, and these people, his supporting cast, have been very important to his success.

—Walt "Ozz" Ostrowski,
Head boys basketball coach at
Hatboro-Horsham High

Jameer (in the 2000 PIAA championship game) goes for a steal.

Looking at the sea of orange and black shirts all around the huge Hershey Arena, it seemed like the whole town of Chester must have come to the state finals. Led by the fast rhythm and foot stomping of their outstanding cheerleaders, there was incredible spirit and excitement in the air. The intensity with which the Clippers played continued into the celebration after they won the championship.

Rob Knox, who had followed Jameer and the team as sportswriter for the local Delaware *Daily Times*, described it perfectly: "And boy did the

Clippers party. As the final buzzer sounded, the Clipper players were swallowed under a mob of jubilant Chester fans and being showered with Hershey Kisses at the same time."

More than anything about that final championship game, however, his father remembers Jameer running into the stands when the victory over Uniontown was theirs, scooping up his then-eight-year old brother Maurice, jumping and down with him in his arms and then taking him on a celebration run around the court. To see the two of them this way filled his heart with incredible joy.

Fred remembers that Pete was always there for all the games, even in the summer. He would pile the boys into his old red "Sanford & Son" truck to help transport them to their games. He did not try to intercede with the coaching, preferring to stay in the background. After the games, he would treat everyone to ice creams and sodas. It was clear that he was there not only for Jameer, but for all the kids...in Fred's words, "a 100 percent genuine person."

Adding to the honor of leading his team to the state championship, Jameer was named to Pennsylvania's first-team all-state for high school boys basketball. At the conclusion of his high school years, his statistics were these: an average of six rebounds, seven assists and 21 points per game.

The 2000 PIAA

*Jameer shoots during the 2000 PIAA
championship game against Uniontown.*

Championship

Fred Pickett giving Jameer his medal for the 2000 PIAA championship.

Naeem Scott (left), Lateef Watts (center) and Jameer celebrating their 2000 PIAA championship.

Jameer (playing defense in a high school game against Williamsport) always gave 100 percent no matter what.

Not seen on the stat charts, however, were the immeasurable leadership skills and confidence he had developed at Chester High School.

Adding to Chester's pride, Fred was named Pennsylvania's 1999-2000 Big-School Boys' Basketball Coach of the Year. As Jameer's high school career was coming to its close, Fred said: "He stacks up there with some of the best that have ever played for Chester High. I am going to miss him, but he is just beginning. Even bigger things are ahead for him, and his story is far from being finished."

One of the honors Jameer received, starting in his junior year, was to be invited to play in the Donofrio Classic, for many years the most renowned postseason tournament for high school players in the Philadelphia area. It was here that college coaches and what are known as the "basketball junkies" gather each year to see the best of the best in the Philadelphia area. Jameer played, along with Pat Carroll (from Hatboro-Horsham and later his teammate at Saint Joseph's), Bennie Stewart (from Glen Mills and then Hutchinson Junior College), Mark Lester (from Harrisburg and then Morgan State), and his Chester High teammates Lateef Watts, Naeem Scott (later at Lincoln University), and Ray Strickland (later at Alvernia College) on the Mainstreet Systems team sponsored by Mike Galante and Chuck and Elaine

DIDJA HEAR 'BOUT JAMEER?

NELSON WAS CLEARLY the top player in Delaware County this season. The senior guard averaged 20.8 points, seven assists, six rebounds and four steals per game. Those numbers don't begin to describe the impact he had for the Clippers (24-4), who are still alive in their bid to capture a PIAA Class AAAA state championship. Nelson wowed fans throughout the county with his deceptive quickness, brute strength, deft shooting touch, the heart of a winner and his beautiful ball handling.

When the Del-Val League coaches gather to pick their 1999-2000 All-Del Val team for the season, one player stood out above the rest. Chester High's Jameer Nelson was a unanimous choice as the Del Val League Player of the Year.

—Rob Knox,
sportswriter for the *Delco Times*,
near the end of Jameer's senior season

Whelan. He asked for, and was granted, No. 14 for every year he played on this team. Even when Mainstreet's team did not make it to the finals, Jameer was elected to the all-tournament team.

One of the memorable highlights from his high school days was getting invited to the prestigious Dapper Dan Classic in Pittsburgh. Jameer stayed into the evening to play with Mainstreet's Donofrio team and then hopped into a van to travel with his coaches, Fred and Keddy, and his father Pete, driving all the way to what they came to consider his first big event. At the Dapper Dan were young basketball players from all over the world. Those from Yugoslavia told Jameer that with his skills, he would be paid to play in their country, and they invited him to come to Yugoslavia. It was here that Jameer was first called "the best point guard in the country," but at the conclusion of the tournament, he did not get elected MVP (Most Valuable Player). Jameer took it in stride, never becoming angry or jealous. This same year, many thought he would be elected as an All-America player, but again the highest awards were not coming his way.

It was in high school that Jameer started lifting weights just enough to stay in shape and be strong, but not too bulky. It was also the point at which he was given his first No. 14 jersey. He kept

DIDJA HEAR 'BOUT JAMEER?

WHEN I WAS PLAYING for Scranton Prep, I participated in an open scrimmage at Saint Joseph's University for high school students. While there, I had the opportunity to play the point guard position against Jameer. Although he was moving at the rate of about one hundred miles an hour, he was really kind to me, smiling and giving me words of confidence.

Like him, I had played on Mainstreet's Donofrio team. Through my friendship with the Whelans, I met his father, Pete. Within a few minutes, I understood where Jameer got so many of his great qualities. Both he and his dad are so strong and sturdy, with broad shoulders and a certain toughness. They both are also very polite and cordial with lots of smiles and encouraging words.

I have now graduated from Scranton Prep and will be headed to Holy Cross University in Worcester, Massachusetts, on a full scholarship next year where I hope I can someday measure up to Jameer. I don't know if anyone can match Jameer's tremendous abilities, but it's going to be fun trying.

—Pat Doherty, basketball player,
All-Pennsylvania AAA First Team,
Robert Larkin Award Winner

Jameer (in his junior year) developed
into a great unselfish point guard.

this number each year and took this number as his whenever he could.

And how did he come to be a point guard? If you could handle the ball really well, you were likely to be given a shot at the point guard position. Jameer could do this at age five and could outmaneuver the seven year olds, so it was only natural he would be a point guard. In these early days, Coach Naeem told him his job was to "pass first, score last" and that basketball was a team, not an individual, sport. When some would urge Jameer to shoot the ball more, he would say, "No, it's my job to give the ball."

In Jameer's sophomore year when Chester was playing Academy Park, Monte Ross, one of the assistant coaches at Saint Joseph's University, was there to see one of the Academy Park players. Fred sat with him and told him Chester had someone very special and he should look at him now. Monte said at the end of the game: "You're right, Coach. We'll be back."

Fred Pickett later called Phil Martelli and recommended he come out to one of the Chester games to see this up-and-coming point guard. Fred told Phil that Jameer was a special young man who could distribute the ball and he was good. Phil later recalled it was Jameer's junior year and a game in which he took no shots and had no points when he first watched him play. But there

"His eyes—they burn with a level of concentration and competitiveness that I have seen in only a few young men." —Jerry Wainwright, head coach, University of Richmond.

was something about the way he dominated the game at both ends that caught Phil's eye. Once he came out to see Jameer, Phil would be at the Chester games as often as NCAA rules would allow, along with the Whelans and Mike Galante. All of them recognized early on that there was something very special about this young player.

DIDJA HEAR 'BOUT JAMEER?

WHEN I WAS SETTING up Hometown Hoops Classic, my first event on January 2, 2000, I wanted to make sure Chester and Jameer Nelson were in it. First, as a Temple guy, I was hoping that John Chaney would continue to have an interest. Second, though I had the game everyone in the city wanted to see in Roman Catholic and Camden, I knew that Jameer was a very special player, too.

It was not an accident that Chester played in that game. It seems funny now that Camden-Roman was played before 9,300 people and that Chester-Pennsbury was played in front of maybe 3,000. Those who remember the little 5-11 guard jump from what seemed like half-court to dunk will never forget it. Jameer stole the show in game one. He was great.

Jameer was also in one of the commercials we made leading up to the game. It was a funny commercial with the guys from Hometown Hoops. Eddie Griffen, Jameer, Arthur Barclay from Camden, and two starters from Pennsbury were on the floor in pajamas and in sleeping bags, actually pretending to be sleeping on the Apollo floor. Jameer's eyes were closed when we pre-taped and later we dubbed him saying, "I wonder if Coach Pickett could get Chester a game here." It was awesome.

—Jeremy Treatman,
Scholastic play-by-play

Jameer's trademark #14 was first given to him at Chester High School.

When it was the appropriate time, according to NCAA rules, Phil came out to Linda's home in Chester to talk about the possibility of Jameer coming to Saint Joseph's University. Pete, Linda, Jameer and the whole family gathered together for the occasion. One of the most memorable moments during this visit came when Phil pulled out a giant size Saint Joseph's University diploma and told Jameer that he could earn one of these, albeit a much smaller size.

Phil, with his down-to-earth manner and easy-going personality, did a wonderful job selling the Nelson family on the merits of coming to Saint Joseph's. He assured them he would have good food, a tutor if needed, and would be close to home. His family told Jameer that they liked the idea of being able to come to his games and to have him able to come home whenever he needed a good home-cooked meal or became ill.

When Jameer decided to go to Saint Joseph's, Pete asked Phil where his first college game would be. Phil responded Colorado and, he remembers, Pete got up from his seat and asked around the room how many would like to go to Colorado. Eleven said yes that night. It was the first of many games where his family and friends would gather as many tickets as they could to be there for him.

Jameer had received many letters from colleges interested in having him come. They offered

Jameer waiting for the press conference to announce his selection of Saint Joseph's University outside the Chester High School gym.

to send plane tickets, to have his parents come along for a school visit, but Phil Martelli was the only one who came to Jameer and his family.

The other college in the Philadelphia area that had been interested in Jameer was Temple University. Four years later, head coach John Chaney was quoted as saying that if he knew then what he knew now, he would have come himself to Jameer's games rather than sending his assistants.

And five years later, remembering Fred Pickett's words about Jameer his junior year, Phil Martelli said: "He wasn't good—he was great!"

CHAPTER 4

Excellence with Commitment

Although his team had won the state championship for its class and he was named to the first-team all-state team, Jameer was not an overly recruited college candidate. Wanting to stay within easy travel distance from his home in Chester, his final choices were narrowed to Temple University and Saint Joseph's University. Both were located in Philadelphia, both were part of the Atlantic 10 Conference.

Temple University was an inner-city school with a number of outlying campuses and a very large student body. Its head coach, John Chaney, and the basketball program were well known with numerous records of success at the national level. Saint Joseph's, in comparison, was a tiny Jesuit Catholic school located in the Overbrook section of the city near the older Main Line suburbs. Its head coach, Phil Martelli, had experienced three losing seasons and was expected to have a fair-to-middling season in the upcoming Atlantic 10.

Why did he choose Saint Joseph's? Jameer liked their fast-paced style, he thought the personal style he had developed would be a good fit. He also liked the experienced players who would be his teammates and believed he could learn from them. In his words, "The definition of a point guard is to get your teammates involved first. You pass and play defense before looking for your shot. The point guard has to do all the dirty stuff. I get excited if I make a nice pass to a teammate who makes a back cut and dunks the ball. That gets me excited, although I don't show it."

But excited and showing it was Phil Martelli, once Jameer told him his choice was St. Joe's. He did not hold back in telling the world about his terrific new recruit, saying Jameer was the "most polished freshman" he had ever recruited since becoming head coach.

Saint Joseph's motto is "Excellence with Commitment" and from both the university and Jameer, this proved to be a common philosophy. Jameer came ready to do all he could to help his teammates win and to continue to develop his academic and basketball skills. The university, from its leaders to its professors to its coaches, held to

Jameer dribbles the ball during his freshman year against the University of Massachusetts Minutemen. (Al Bello/Getty Images)

its motto to do all that it could to support and cheer on the amazing 18 year old who had chosen to come there.

It did not take long for the older, more experienced basketball players to recognize the value of this incoming freshman. From star guard Marvin O'Connor, then a junior, came these words: "He's not your typical freshman. He's very poised, very calm, and he has a lot of skill and confidence. He can also knock down the open shot and he can penetrate, and that's going to open up things for the rest of us. He's in your face on defense. He's been comfortable with us from his first day here. He's just what we needed."

Phil Martelli had promised Pete Nelson that he would be a father to Jameer if this were needed at St. Joe's. Pete had said to him: "My son is in your hands. Treat him like your son." Phil soon had the opportunity to carry through this promise. He was handed a note saying Jameer had cut a class. Before the start of the team's next practice, he told Jameer he would not be able to participate that day and, in addition, he would be sent home. Jameer apologized to Phil before that practice, then called from his cell phone to again apologize and then called Phil at home that evening to apologize for the third time. And he never cut a class again.

For the season opener of Jameer's freshman year, the team traveled to Nashville, Tennessee, to face Western Carolina in the America's Youth Classic tournament. Marvin O'Connor was their top gun, scoring 23 points, but there were contributions all around from senior Erick Woods (16 points), junior forward Bill Phillips (15 points, 11 rebounds), senior Frank Wilkins (11 points) and Damian Reid (four points). The new freshman, Tyrone Barley, gave them six assists and Jameer had eight. The sum total was a 50-point victory (103-53). For the Nelsons, it was looking good, looking like Jameer had made the right choice.

In early February, St. Joe's faced St. Bonaventure's, and Jameer once again faced his high school rival, Marques Green. With just 22 seconds to go in regulation play, St. Bonnie's was leading by five. In an incredible turn of events, Marvin O'Connor was fouled and made both shots, reducing Bonaventure's lead to three. With less than five seconds left, Marques Green was fouled but missed both shots. After getting the rebound, Erick Woods hesitated only a second before getting the ball into Jameer's hands. Jameer raced down the court, stopped at about 30 feet and put up the ball to score three more points to tie the game. Then St. Joe's kept their momentum and went on to win one of the most memorable games of the season, 104-97.

In the Atlantic 10 conference, Temple University is often viewed as the team to beat. In Philadelphia's Big Five, which includes both Saint Joseph's and Temple, the rivalry is always intense. Earlier in the season, St. Joe's Hawks beat the Temple Owls, and there was no doubt in anyone's mind that the Owls would be gunning for them. The Hawks did their homework, shut down Temple's match-up zone and went on to win 71-62. To add to the celebration of this evening, Marvin O'Connor scored the 1,000th point of his college career.

In early March, there was an incredible indelible minute, one few who saw it will ever forget. It was in the game against LaSalle. St. Joe's was down by 10 as the game approached regulation. Then Marvin O'Connor started a run likely to go down in NCAA history as one of the best. Fed by Jameer, he hit three three-pointers, then was fouled and made the three free throws, made two lay-ups for four more points and was fouled again. He made the next two free throws, tallying a grand total of 18 points in one minute. LaSalle was able to overcome this spectacular run with sharp shooting of their own and a final three-pointer at the two-second mark to win 91-90.

At the end of Jameer's freshman year, the Saint Joseph's Hawks basketball team had achieved 25 wins with just 6 losses. After a heart-stopping win over LaSalle in the Atlantic 10 play-offs, they received one of the at-large bids to NCAA Tournament and were given a nine-seed in the NCAA West Regional being held in San Diego. In the NCAA Tournament, the seeds of the initial matches add up to 17, so St. Joe's first played the eight seed, which in 2001 was Georgia Tech.

This was Jameer's first game in what is known as the "Big Dance" and he, together with upper-classmen Na'im Crenshaw, Marvin O'Connor, Bill Phillips, Damien Reid and Frank Wilkins, led their team past Georgia Tech to the second round. One of the newspapers added still another nick-name for Jameer, calling him "Baby Face." In the second round, they met a more formidable oppo-nent in top-seeded Stanford University. Despite Jameer's near triple-double counts in assists, rebounds and points, St. Joe's did not make it to the third round.

With his single-season high of 213 assists, Jameer ranked No. 1 in the Atlantic 10 conference and No. 13 nationally across all conferences. His impact on the high level of success for his team was recognized as Jameer was named Atlantic 10 Rookie of the Year and *Sports Illustrated's* National Freshman of the Year. Each year colorful basket-ball commentator Dick Vitale chooses a new young player to be his "Diaper Dandy" of the year and in 2001 his choice was Jameer Nelson.

It was during his son's freshman year, that Pete Nelson, on his way to a game, spotted a penny on the street, dirty and most likely run over by a number of cars. For reasons still unknown to him, Pete picked it up and put it in his pocket. That night, in a crunch game, St. Joe's won. He dubbed it his "lucky penny" and moved it, along with his tiny church key (military can opener) from Vietnam, to his wallet for safekeeping. He would not go to a game without it and has said that even if offered $10,000 for it, he would not part with it. Whenever St. Joe's has been in a tight spot, as they were in the next-to-last conference game with Rhode Island in Jameer's final year, he puts the penny in his hand and holds on tight. Almost always it worked, as it did that night!

Whenever he could break away from his work, Pete found a way to attend his son's games home and away from the time he was in elementary school through his high school years and then college. And whenever time permitted, he would buy a grill and the ingredients to make his special barbeques for the team while they were on the road. He recalls, among other locales, cooking for them in New Orleans, Louisiana, Wichita, Kansas, Evansville, Indiana, and Cocoa Beach, Florida.

When it came time to pick a college major, Jameer chose sociology. His mentor, Earl Pearsall's son Ernest, had also chosen Saint Joseph's University and a major in sociology. Older than Jameer, Ernest graduated with a bachelor's degree and went on to become an advisor for a college basketball team in New York. Each year, Jameer continued his studies through the summer months, filling in whatever he needed to keep his grades high. Many of his professors were impressed with this dedication, telling Pete Nelson his son was a "class act," and they wanted to help him succeed.

Evenings would find Jameer playing for the Earl Foster team in the PureGames League held at the Tri-States Sports facility in Aston near his home. This league had developed into what many considered to be the best summer action in and around the Philadelphia area, attracting even professional players wanting to keep up their skills in the off season. For those who could no longer get in-season tickets to see Jameer play with the Saint Joseph's Hawks, this was the place to be. Three of the regulars were his father, Pete, and his friends, Chuck and Elaine Whelan, and it was here that the idea for this book was born.

During the summer of 2001, Jameer was one of 12 players invited to play on the 2001 USA Basketball World Championship for Young Men

DIDJA HEAR 'BOUT JAMEER?

JAMEER HAS PLAYED in the *PureGame Media Men's Summer League since he was in the 10th grade. Chester High always entered a team in the league to play the best competition. On one particular night when Jameer was a 10th grader, Furillo's Steak Shop (Chester's sponsor for the league) was playing Cabrini College. Young Jameer scored 33 points, dished out 10 assists, and five rebounds against a very good Division III basketball team. I knew that night that Jameer was special. He was quiet and humble about his performance. The very next game, he made sure all of his teammates scored.*

Each summer, I would talk to Jameer about his jump shot and, lo and behold after working hard, the Lord blessed him to be able to shoot with major players. Jameer always worked hard to be the best.

—Pastor Stephen Michael Lewis,
Director of PureGame Media Men's
Summer League

*Jameer and Marvin O'Connor pose for a picture
during practice in October 2001. (AP/WWP)*

Team in the 2001 World Championship for
Young Men tournament being held in Saitama,
Japan. This was a spectacular adventure for Jameer
with travel to a distant country with a culture
quite different from the one he had known. The
basketball courts were not so different, however,
and Jameer helped the USA team, coached by Jim
Boeheim of Syracuse, win its first eight games to
reach the finals. And then they went on to win it
all and come home with gold medals. To add to
the celebration, Jameer was coming home to meet
his just-born son, Jameer Jr.

As Jameer moved on to his sophomore year, excitement was building at St. Joe's, known in the local area as Hawk Hill. Although they had not been nationally ranked since the mid-1960s, they were picked as No. 10 in the preseason rankings.

Returning proven players included senior Bill Phillips, known for his sound fundamentals and excellent rebounding, sophomore Tyrone Barley, known for sharp shooting and fierce defense, and sophomore John Bryant, who was developing into a fine forward. Center Alexandre Sazanov, now a junior, was returning to the lineup after leg surgery.

Delonte West, with an excellent high-school record and an Atlantic 10 preseason pick for the All-Rookie squad, was a new addition with great potential. Also coming on board were Dwayne Jones, a star player from Chester, and sharp-shooter Pat Carroll, who had played with Jameer on the Mainstreet team and factored continuing to play with him into his college decision. Phil Martelli looked forward to his next season coaching these players, saying: "This place is cooking with excitement. We could have sold every season ticket two times over."

From the time they first played together, Jameer and Bill Phillips were very much in sync both as friends and on the court. Jameer played the point guard position, Bill the forward. Bill's

DIDJA HEAR 'BOUT JAMEER?

WE RECRUITED JAMEER NELSON when I was at Hofstra—I thought he could replace Speedy Claxton. We thought we found a sleeper. Then the Hawks jumped in and it was over.

The next time I saw Jameer was when we played Saint Joseph's at the Pavilion during his sophomore year. We won the game handily. I looked at Jameer when the game was getting out of hand. He was a sophomore following the lead of seniors. He was by far the best player. I told my staff after the game, "This isn't going to happen again. Next year that will be Jameer's team."

—Jay Wright,
Head basketball coach,
Villanova University

parents were French and both had played professional basketball. Bill was tall, but not quite as tall as his father, who measured seven feet.

Bill's mother, as well as his sister, rode the parents' bus along with the Nelsons. Pete recalls she would say "Aw man, there's nothing to drink on this bus…no vodka!" and make everyone laugh.

Although Jameer's reputation as a ball player was good and growing stronger, there were moments of despair, moments of discouragement, moments when basketball rivalries became ugly. Pete recalled the game against St. Bonaventure in Jameer's junior year. It was Senior Night at the Reilly Center in Olean, New York, and packed with St. Bonnie's fans. There were calls to "Kill the Bird" and then an attempted tackle on the Hawk, St. Joe's mascot.

When Jameer threw in the last shot to win the game, St. Bonnie's fans threw their cups of soda and trash at him. Their premier point guard, Marques Green, of course. was Jameer's biggest rival. Even though they did not meet head to head in regular play, some fans and analysts would say Marques was the better of the two, while others said it was Jameer. Once, when Pete told the guy in the stands next to him that Jameer was his son, he was told: "Well, Marques is going to tear him apart."

Jameer hugs coach Phil Martelli after being taken out of the St. Bonnie's game on March 2, 2004. (AP/WWP)

Then just one year later, when St. Joe's was again playing St. Bonnie's and winning by more than 50 points, Jameer was taken out of the game with 19 minutes to go so that another St. Joe's point guard could have more time on the floor. This time, the St. Bonnie's crowd cheered Jameer,

The St. Joe's team members, starting from left, John Bryant, Dwayne Jones, Jameer, Dwayne Lee, and Tyrone Bailey react as they are picked as a No. 7 seed in the 2003 NCAA tournament. (AP/WWP)

giving him a big round of applause. Marques issued words of praise for his old-time rival.

Both Pete and his good friend, Calvin Bernard, remember heading north on the turnpike to Scranton, Pennsylvania, in Pete's little red truck, known by everyone as the "Sanford & Son" truck. Holes developed in the hose, all of the fluid drained out, and the truck overheated. Even though it was old, this was the first time it had broken down. Fortunately, however, this happened right in front of the state troopers barracks. They came out to help them, gave them water, and Pete and Calvin were repaired sufficiently to be on their way again. As they were leaving, one of the troopers said "Is that truck legal?" and laughed. The guys made it to Jameer's game just in time.

In Jameer's junior year, St. Joe's finished with 23 wins, just six losses and was once again invited to the NCAA tournament. Playing against Auburn with Delonte West hurt and out of action, St. Joe's was neck-and-neck near the end. Jameer had hit three three-pointers in a row and tallied 33 points, but it was to no avail as they lost by one shot.

CHAPTER 5

Jameer Starts His Own Family

During his freshman year in college, Jameer was dating Imani Tillery who, had graduated from Chester High School and was attending Temple University. When she learned a baby was on the way, there were natural "uh-oh" feelings on the part of everyone close to them. Would this end their college goals? Would Jameer have to stop playing ball?

But courtesy of the good values of the Nelson and Tillery families, initial fears were soon put to rest. Jameer would look forward to being a father, Imani to being a mother and somehow, just as they have always done, the families would welcome this new addition and help in any way they could.

Imani went into labor just when Jameer and the USA team were entering the finals for the World Games being held in Japan in August of 2001. Jameer was torn between trying to come home in time to see the baby being born and finishing up the games, and there were many calls back and forth trying to figure out what to do. Not knowing exactly when the baby would arrive and whether he could be there in time, he decided to finish the final game and then come home as quickly as possible.

The birth went fine, Jameer was able to be in touch by telephone, and a beautiful baby boy named Jameer Jr. arrived.

Plans were made so both parents could finish college, Jameer could continue with his basketball and to give their son, soon nicknamed Meer-meer, plenty of love and attention.

During school days, Jameer's older sister Althea has Meer-meer at her daycare center, where she gives him special attention to learn the ABCs and to count. On weekdays, when her school day is done, Imani cares for her son. On weekends, Jameer's mother Linda, and her husband John Billings, alternate with Jameer's father Pete, and his wife Elsie, to have Meer-meer with them whenever they are needed. Jameer opens up as much time as possible to be with his son wherever he is.

For most of Jameer's games, someone in the family brings Meer-meer to the game and then, when it is over and friends and fans gather around, little Meer-meer is right there in his daddy's arms. They have learned, however, to sit up a little bit higher in the stands, because if Meer-meer is close to the action, he wants to jump right into the game to be with his father.

Imani's father, George, had also played basketball at Chester High School, further giving Jameer Jr. quite a legacy. Jameer's father had come from a family with six sons, all athletic and interested in sports. In addition to Pete, the Nelson brothers included Anthony, Duke, Lloyd, James and Johnny. Although their sports were primarily baseball and basketball, Lloyd as a middleweight boxer participated in the 1968 Olympics in Mexico and was the top middleweight in Philadelphia.

All the early signs are that Jameer Jr. not only looks very much like his father, but possesses many of his qualities. He is said to be very persistent when he wants something. At two, he jumps and dribbles a standard-size basketball with a skill far beyond his years and does not want to stop. Pete recalls telling his son many times "This is your last shot," and then after he shot 10 more times, he would have to say again, "This is your

last shot," and on it went. And now Jameer Sr.
finds himself doing the same thing with Jameer Jr.

At the crucial Rhode Island game, near the
end of Jameer's senior season, Meer-meer was in
attendance, standing near the Rhode Island coaches with Pete, Elijah Holmes and Jamie, a friend
from Chester High. With his jumping, he cap-
tured the attention of the Rhode Island coaches.
The coaches started laughing and seemed to be
paying less mind to the game and more to the tod-
dler. At one point, one of the coaches said, "Man,
we could really use him."

Meer-meer has become used to seeing his
father playing in games, both live and on television, and will point out to whoever happens to be
around, "That's my daddy!" He also knows how to
"do the Hawk," running and flapping his arms
just like Saint Joseph's renowned mascot.

When games, tournaments and awards have
taken Jameer to distant places, he has said that
what he most looks forward to is coming home to
be with his son.

In the Nelson family, there is a ten-year gap
between Jameer and his younger brother Maurice,
and then another ten-year gap between Maurice
and Meer-meer. Maurice has shown exceptional
ability in both baseball and basketball and is saying that someday he, too, will be at Saint Joseph's.
We are guessing that in the years ahead, both Pete

and Jameer Sr. will be spending many hours taking the younger Nelsons to and from practices, to and from games, and most likely to and from award banquets.

CHAPTER 6

Should He Stay or Head to the NBA?

In the spring of Jameer's junior year at Saint Joseph's University, he was invited to participate in the NBA (National Basketball Association) predraft camp being held at the Moody Bible Institute in Chicago in early June. His name had been submitted by Saint Joseph's University and then met with approval from the NBA committee for underclassmen.

Recent changes in NBA rules allowed college underclassman to participate in the draft. Once a player officially declares himself eligible for the draft, he can no longer return to play in NCAA (National Collegiate Athletic Association) games for his college. The rules also stipulated that in order to attend the predraft camp with the option to return to school, a player could not be signed with an agent. The camp works in two ways, one to have each player work with the other leading contenders for the draft to see how well they compare, and the other to have the NBA scouts take a closer look at each player. For the player, it means an all-expenses paid trip and an opportunity to compete.

In the time from completion of the camp up until about one week before the draft, each player who has not signed with an agent can make the decision to return to his former situation or to declare himself in contention for the NBA draft, which is held each year in late June.

Jameer decided to explore this opportunity and traveled to Chicago with assistant coach Monte Ross from St. Joe's. By all accounts, he performed very well with seven assists, 13 points and no turnovers. He was included in the list of 11 players who got the best of play during their week in Chicago with this NBA report from Chris Ekstrand:

"The Numbers: 10.3 ppg, 6.3 apg, 54.5 FG%, 87.5 FT%.

The Performance: Nelson, the fireplug point guard who was the engine of Saint Joseph's offense the past couple of seasons, gave a fine accounting of his abilities at the camp. Those who had not spent much time scouting the Atlantic 10 in recent years might have been surprised, but East Coast scouts knew what Nelson would do: make the open shot when it presented itself, get his teammates in position to run the play correctly in half-court sets, and penetrate and distribute the ball with very few turnovers. Nelson basically answered all the questions any NBA teams might have about his game, all in the affirmative. The only thing holding Nelson back is something he can't do anything about: his height (6-0). Nelson is a junior who can go back to school if he chooses."

In the predraft camp, however, 2003 came to be known as the year of the point guard. Competing with Jameer was Boston College's Troy Bell, who was Player of the Year in the Big East Conference and a second-team All-American. Troy drew rave reviews for his performance at the camp, with seven assists, 17 points and a tournament high of four steals. Several other point guards who performed well included Alexander Vujaciic from Slovakia and Carl English from Hawaii. All had the advantage of greater height than Jameer, who was just a shade less than six feet.

Since the field of excellent point guards was large and there was concern that Jameer might not be tall enough to do well in the NBA, the word coming from the NBA scouts was that it was a possibility, but not a strong one, that he would be picked in the first round. Although there is a second round and then the possibility of individual tryouts with specific teams, only those who are selected in the first round of the draft are guaranteed a contract.

Those close to him, his teammates, his coaches, and many other basketball fans followed news from the Chicago camp closely and anxiously waited for what became known as "The Decision" from Jameer. He returned to the Philadelphia area with his mind still not made up. Each day, newscasters would broadcast the news: "No decision yet." He later said: "It was really close, between the NBA or college."

He consulted with a number of people who had been close to him, including family, friends and coaches, who helped him weigh the alternatives of NBA status and money versus getting a college degree and the possibility of setting new records at Saint Joseph's. The first person he officially told was his Saint Joseph's coach Phil Martelli, and the answer was yes, he would be coming back to school. Together, coach and player cooked up a little bit of fun and called for a team meeting. In Saint Joseph's basketball office, Jameer stood in front of his teammates and

DIDJA HEAR 'BOUT JAMEER?

MY STRONGEST MEMORY of Jameer was from the district playoffs with Hatboro-Horsham High School. He took a fadeaway jumper right at the buzzer and made it, winning the game for Chester High. He was a clutch player, and this was another example of how he would come through when it was most needed.

I had seen Marques Green play with Norristown High when he was a junior, and at that time thought he was the better player. In my profession, we tend to pitch players based on what we see at a particular point in their lives and not always on what happens next. Although he was not a McDonald's All-American, what Jameer did was work uncommonly hard every year and progressively he became better and better. He became an example of how to do things the right way.

When Tim Duncan was a sophomore at Wake Forest, the consensus was that he could be the first player selected in the NBA draft. He elected not to do this and went on

*to graduate before signing up to play profes-
sional basketball. He was selected as MVP
and is now considered by many to be the
most complete player. In a world where so
many young players want instant gratifica-
tion, what Tim and Jameer did in choosing
not to skip steps, in choosing to play college
ball and go on to graduate, provides the
best role model.*

—Tom Konchalski,
Basketball Analyst, HSBI
(High School Basketball Index)

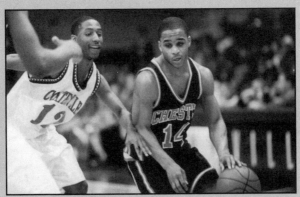

*Jameer's dazzling play and accomplish-
ments will no doubt be added to the
rich tradition of Chester
basketball.*

declared to them that his decision was to go with the draft. According to Tyrone Barley, who had come on board the team the same year as Jameer, "We all bought it. Everybody sat there like somebody died."

With precise timing, Jameer continued on and let everyone know his real decision—to return to play with them another year. In addition to lots of laughter, there were huge sighs of relief.

Jameer said: "At some times, I was almost there. But there were things I felt I could accomplish, as far as school and my team. I felt I needed to be a Hawk." He later added: "You're taking a chance entering the draft, and you're taking a chance coming back. I wanted to make a decision because of me being happy. And I'm probably one of the happiest people playing basketball right now."

Even coaches from competing teams who would have fared better had Jameer removed himself from college ball expressed happiness at his return. In November of 2003, coach Mark Few whose Gonzaga team was scheduled to play against St. Joe's the following day said to Jameer: "Thanks for coming back. You're special to the sport of college basketball."

Jameer entered his senior year determined to have fun and take on the challenge of accomplishing an even greater season with his Saint Joseph's teammates. In still another interview, he said: "What did it come down to? Whether I wanted to be in the real world or still be a kid."

And no matter what happened on the basketball court, he and his parents would be proud that he would be earning a college degree.

"The Decision" would come to be known as one of the best ever.

CHAPTER 7

Senior Year ... What a Year

For many among his family, friends and fans, there was great joy that there would be a senior year for Jameer. He had given serious consideration to entering the NBA after a terrific junior year in which he established himself as one of the most premier players in the country. He decided to stay. He wanted one more year with his college teammates, and they and all his fans wanted one more year to be with him. From all quarters, it was considered a good thing that he would be earning his bachelor's degree from Saint Joseph's University.

From his coach Phil Martelli came these words: "I've said all along that Jameer is the best point guard in America, but he is an even better person. He cares so much about his school, his

Jameer laughs as he catches a pass during practice in his senior season at St. Joe's. (AP/WWP)

teammates and this program that no one should be surprised with his decision. He is coming back to school for all the right reasons, and his legacy will be like those left by Tim Duncan, Grant Hill, Lionel Simmons, and David West, four-year guys with tremendous character."

Returning with Jameer were two other starters from the prior season, Pat Carroll and Delonte West. Jameer had been co-captain his junior year and would share the role this year with senior

DIDJA HEAR 'BOUT JAMEER?

HAVING COACHED AGAINST Jameer and being a veteran coach of 37 years, I can say without reservation that he is one of the most intense, focused and team-oriented young men that I have seen compete in the game of basketball. What I will always remember about him are his eyes—they burn with a level of concentration and competitiveness that I have seen in only a few young men, the most notable being Tim Duncan, who I worked with at Wake Forest University.

Jameer sees the game "a play ahead," and because of that the team always becomes more important than any individual achievements.

—Jerry Wainwright,
Head Basketball Coach,
University of Richmond

Tyrone Barley, who had been sixth man. Now a junior, Delonte West would be in the two-guard position to carry on their run as the best backcourt duo in collegiate basketball.

Also back and ready for an even bigger role would be Pat Carroll who, when he was at Hatboro-Horsham High School, played against Jameer who was at Chester High. After regular-season play, they would again run into competition each year in the district playoffs. Saint Joseph's coaches had been interested in Pat's older brother, Matt, and had come to know the whole Carroll family. Matt chose to go to Notre Dame to play, but Pat became interested in St. Joe's and they in him. Pat and Jameer became teammates rather than competitors when they played together for two years on Mainstreet's team in the Donofrio postseason tournament. When Pat was making his college choice, his father, John, said that he factored playing with Jameer into his decision, and that he had said, "If you can't beat him, then join him." Like his older brother, Pat became known as an extraordinary sharp shooter, a sweet shooter. In his prior season, Pat had been the leading three-point percentage shooter in the nation.

Jameer's senior classmate, Tyrone Barley, had proven himself as a reliable sixth man in the prior 2002-2003 season and was ready to move up to a starting position. Junior center Dwayne Jones,

John Bryant (left), Jameer (center) and Delonte West (right) celebrate another win during the 2003-2004 season. (AP/WWP)

also hailing from Chester, had been a high-impact player both for points and rebounds. Another junior, John Bryant, like Tyrone, had provided excellent backup defense and was ready to move up to a larger role. Three sophomores—Dwayne Lee, Dave Mallon and Chet Stachitas—had played significant minutes and provided excellent backup support. They had all developed a unity, worked hard on new defensive measures and knew how to effectively play together.

Four team members as well as the team were given preseason honors by the Atlantic 10 Conference. Jameer and Delonte West were named to the Preseason All-Conference Team, and

Pat Carroll was named to the third team. Jameer and Dwayne Jones were named to the All-Defensive Team. Saint Joseph's was picked to be the No. 1 team in the East, Xavier in the West division.

When the preseason basketball magazines hit the stands, there was Jameer on the cover of *Basketball Times* captioned with "He's Back!" It was a clean sweep as he had earned first-team All-America status in all of the preseason publications and was slated to be a candidate for National Player of the Year. Sports commentator Dick Vitale named him to his Second Rolls Royce Team. These teams cite those players considered best in their position for the upcoming year. Early in the season Vitale again cited Jameer as an electrifying player with tremendous passion for the game. Then, early in the new calendar year, Vitale said his choice for player of year at that moment would be the little dynamite backcourt sensation at St. Joe's—Jameer Nelson. He added that, pound for pound and inch for inch, Jameer was the best pure talent in the nation.

In November, ESPN.com asked Jameer to be part of their *Timeout Chat Show* where fans could send in their questions regarding the upcoming season and have them personally answered by Jameer.

DIDJA HEAR 'BOUT JAMEER?

JAMEER NELSON REALLY is a young guy who is a winner. He has a special mental tenacity that separates him from many who have played the game on a collegiate level. He defies all odds, as many critics have stated over the years that he is too small to really be special. Well, he proved them wrong on a collegiate level, as he became the best player in the entire nation, and he will prove the critics wrong at the NBA level, because this young guy flat-out has game, has quick skills and most of all has a special sense of pride that separates him from many who play the game.

A consummate winner and a genuine team-oriented player!

—Dick Vitale,
sports commentator for ESPN,
author of *Living a Dream*

With a large following of high-spirited fans, they opened up their season by playing a fellow Jesuit school, Gonzaga University, in the Coaches vs. Cancer Classic at Madison Square Garden in New York. Contests between these two rivals had always resulted in exciting games, and this one was no different. Throughout the game, the score was neck-and-neck, but Saint Joseph's trailed 38-34 at halftime. A revitalized second half put them back on top. Through exceptional teamwork, they kept themselves ahead and conquered the favored Gonzaga 73-66. Jameer was awarded the trophy for Most Valuable Player. Pete Nelson was sitting high in the stands, but Jameer found him and ran up to give his father the trophy and a big, sweaty hug. His son was back and doing just fine. It was a beautiful start to his senior season.

After their opening victory, ESPN.com named Jameer Player of the Week and commented that he was "simply sensational with the basketball, allowing them to create tremendous ball movement." Saint Joseph's was named Team of the Week and cited as the best team in the Coaches vs. Cancer event. For the sixth time, Jameer was named Atlantic 10 Player of the Week. Their national ratings jumped from No. 18 to No. 13 in the *Associated Press* poll, to No.15 in *Sports Illustrated's* poll.

The season marched on with wins against Boston University, Old Dominion, San Francisco, University of Pennsylvania, Boston College, Drexel University, California, University of the Pacific and then University of Delaware in the preseason through to the end of December. Saint Joseph's had reached the 10-0 mark and moved their rank from No. 13 up to No. 10. Jameer calmly told his father, "We're going to continue. We're going to keep on winning."

In early January, Atlantic 10 Conference play began with a victory over George Washington University. Saint Joseph's moved their national ranking from No. 10 to No. 9. The team was more solid then ever, everyone doing their job, playing with excellence and unselfishness. Throughout January, their conference and travel schedules were heavy with most of the games on the road. Victories mounted as they overcame University of Richmond, Duquesne University, Fordham University, Xavier University, University of Massachusetts, St. Bonaventure, and Temple University.

Once when Pete and Jameer were talking, Pete mentioned to Jameer that he saw him at times motioning to the other players to give him the ball back, but they did not, and then they did not succeed in their next play. He said that if it were him, he would be upset. Jameer just smiled and said,

From left: Pat Carroll, Delonte West, Dwayne Jones, coach Phil Martelli, Tyrone Barley, John Bryant and Jameer were ready to win in the 2003-2004 season. (AP/WWP)

"But you aren't me, Dad." Pete recalls that in the next game, when Jameer motioned and got the ball back in his hands, he looked up to him in the stands and cocked his head as if to say, "See, I do get it back."

Their ranking moved up quickly from No. 9 to No. 6 and then No. 3, and their record was still perfect at 18-0. Delonte, Tyrone and Pat were strong, making major contributions to the scoreboard. This was not a team of just a few stars, however. Over the stretch of the season, guys like

John Barley, the two Dwaynes—Jones and Lee, and Chet Stachitas were all catalysts to the tremendous success and cohesion that developed. Although from different backgrounds, they came to share the same goals, the same aspirations, the same mindset, and that was to *win*.

All had come to Saint Joseph's from a winning history and tradition. Tyrone Barley, the self-appointed ladies man of the team, had played at Seton Hall Prep with big names like Brandon Knight and Marcus Toney-El. He was no stranger to winning. Over his four high school years, his teams won New Jersey State Championships and Tournament of Champions titles. He had come to Saint Joseph's unsure of himself as a complete player, but over the course of his college career playing with and against Jameer, he developed into an outstanding talent. Not once, but a number of times, Jameer told reporters and analysts that the hardest opponent he faced was not from another team, but from his own, and that was Tyrone.

Dwayne Lee had come from the storied St. Anthony tradition in New Jersey where winning championships and performing at the highest levels in the most tense situations were commonplace. What he brought to the team were grittiness and leadership by example, something that underclassmen should want and demand of themselves.

Although he played behind the best point guard in the nation, you could never tell by watching him play alongside Jameer. His competition in practice was thought to be a major factor in Jameer's success in game competition.

The other Dwayne was Jones, also known as "DJ." He was shy and reserved off the court, but assumed his alter ego on the floor, dunking with ferocity, tearing the ball out of his opponents' hands. He was half of the frontcourt enforcers whose duty it was to shut down and contain the nation and league's strongest and toughest. Like Jameer, his hometown was Chester, but he attended American Christian Academy in his high school days. There he played center as well as power forward. Training in both areas allowed him to guard players, both larger and smaller than himself, as well as deal with the variances in speed and strength that each different match-up presented. Jameer and Robert Hartshorn were the only players who discovered who the team's "Secret Squirrel" was, the trickster who would put M&Ms in their hat or misplace one of their shoes when they were sleeping. Not a soul suspected it could be the quiet, boy next door DJ.

The suspected practical joker would have been John Bryant, known as the clown prince of the team and the other half of the frontcourt enforcers. He had played with Woodbridge

DIDJA HEAR 'BOUT JAMEER?

I HAVE KNOWN JAMEER since we were both seven and living in Chester. We played on the local baseball, basketball and football teams, mostly of them AAU, until my family and I moved to New Jersey when I was 13. We called him Booby then.

I remember playing his team one night when we were very young. He had 26 points that night. The coaches would say, "Stop this guy, stop this guy." He was very talented for someone so young. He played the last five minutes of the game with as much enthusiasm and vigor as the first. He would cut like Michael Jordan and make these acrobatic maneuvers and plays that no one saw coming. Everyone would wonder how he made those amazing plays.

It wasn't until we met up again at Saint Joseph's that we developed a better friendship. We would both say, "Man, I think this is the best place for me."

After my great-grandmother Robirda Latimore died, my grandfather told me that her greatest wish had been for me to continue to play basketball. I consulted with Jameer about the possibility of joining the team at Saint Joseph's. He said, "Man, you can play," and urged me to try to keep my promise to my great-grandma. I approached the coaches, tried out and then came on board my junior year as a walk-on. He would never admit it, but I think Jameer may have said something to the coaches on my behalf. Whether he did this or simply built my confidence to give it a try, I want to thank Jameer for helping me make my dream and my great-grandma's dream come true.

As soon as I came on the team he did everything to make me feel not just like a teammate but a friend. And in a world filled with as many prima donnas as superstars, it's rare to find a diamond in the rough like Jameer.

—Robert Hartshorn,
former teammate on
Saint Joseph's basketball team

Academy in Virginia and possessed a great many intangibles, such as focus, resourcefulness and aggressiveness. His attitude was one of "never say die…find a way" that expected only the best from himself and his counterparts. In the 2003 conference semifinal against Dayton, there was a loose ball around half court. With two Dayton players within grabbing distance of the ball, John dove and pushed the ball forward to a sprinting Jameer, who then scored a lay-up to authenticate a game-changing rally. John also brought a hearty sense of family and love to the team, always smiling and laughing or making a joke. His fun would be infectious. During practice, he and Jameer would sometimes wrestle and tussle back and forth when they would get matched up against each other and afterwards laugh because of the disproportion of their sizes.

Still another player from a championship background was Leonard Chester Stachitas, better known as "Chet." He was a former state champion high jumper and long jumper from Nease High School, a Florida powerhouse in .Ponte Vedra Beach. Chet was typically very quiet, but then at the most unexpected or ridiculous moment, would dish out facts and flashes of brilliance. He was a slick pure shooter with great mechanics but tended not to create his own shots. Jameer told him to shoot the ball, and began to look for him to receive his passes. Given the opportunity, the extra nudge from Jameer, Chet showed that he could shoot the proverbial lights out. It is expected he will garner a lot of attention from both national and local media as one of the league's top shooters and all-around players in his remaining college years.

Also remarkable about the team was the fact that one-quarter—four of the 16 players—were not recruited players, but "walk-ons." Two of the guys who tried out and won spots for themselves on the team were seniors Robert Hartshorn and Brian Jesiolowski. Here is how Robert put it: "We were all just guys who were living our dream just being a part of this exceptional team. But we also felt it was our obligation to not be satisfied with just being a part of the experience, but to compete on a daily basis as if we were the ones who would be playing in the big games for all the chips."

From when he was seven years old until he moved to New Jersey when he was thirteen, Robert had played with and against Jameer on local Chester teams as well as the AAU national circuit. In his high school years in New Jersey, he played on the nationally ranked prep school team at Faith Christian Academy that competed in the International Preparatory Tournament in Toronto, Canada. As a vocal leader and tireless worker, he helped his team win a ranking in the top 50 prep school teams.

Like Robert, Brian was a walk-on in his junior year and working toward his degree in pharmaceutical marketing. He had played at Lebanon Catholic High School in Pennsylvania and helped them win a district championship. He was one of the team comedians who also led by his strong work ethic and ability to welcome challenges and keep cool in the most heated situations. He and Robert realized how much they had in common and worked together to become excellent students as well as athletes. Brian was named to the deans' athletic honor roll as well as the Atlantic 10 All-Academic Team. There were moments, however, when the two of them were both unsure as to whether they were tough enough to make it through the rigors of being a student athlete on a nationally ranked team whose school enforces very high academic standards. In and through each other, they found the strength and encouragement they needed to not only see themselves through, but to also pass the message on to the next generation of walk-ons who would carry their legacy.

This next generation included two more walk-ons, freshman Andrew Koefer and sophomore Robert Sullivan. Through the media, Andrew became famous as the walk-on who Jameer saved from the ax. Phil Martelli had determined that Andrew would be cut from the team and was about to tell him when a call came in from Jameer asking the coach to give him a chance. Jameer's persuasion was strong enough to make Phil change his mind, and Andrew stayed. He came to be affectionately known as "Hoosier," because he embodied the story that Gene Hackman brought to life in the *Hoosiers* movie about a small-town Indiana team that beat all the odds to win their state championship. In his high school years, he was known as a go-to guy on the Allentown Central Catholic team that went deep into their district playoffs. He carried that same spirit into his first year at Saint Joseph's and this, along with his famous story, embodied what the Jesuit tradition and Saint Joseph's University are all about.

Rob Sullivan brought to his first year at Saint Joseph's a history of success not only as a basketball player but also an all-star soccer player at LaSalle High School in Philadelphia. He was a tenacious player whose drive to win and succeed was overshadowed only by his love for his teammates. Every day in practice he made the starters "earn their pay" with his constant hustle and determination. He also embodied the Jesuit tradition with his heart and integrity on the court as well as one of the highest grade point averages of about 3.7 on a 4.0 scale.

In addition to the walk-ons, the other reserve players who helped make the team so successful were freshmen Artur Surov from Finland, Arvydas Lidzius from Lithuania and Robert Ferguson from Florida. The 2003-2004 team was an intricate set of personalities and talents that fit so well together that, for a time, it was impossible to stop it. Whenever they played in Philadelphia, whether at their own field house or the famed Palestra on the University of Pennsylvania campus, the place was packed not only with people but incredible energy, excitement and enthusiasm. If you could somehow find one, it was the best ticket in Philadelphia.

Every week, more awards and accolades came their way. Jameer was named Atlantic 10 and Big 5 Player of the Week five more times, a candidate for the Bayer Advantage Senior Class Award, named to the Atlantic 10 Silver Anniversary Team by ESPN and then named to the Wooden Award midseason list.

In one of the most memorable games of the season, Delonte West played what is known as a "perfect game" when his team met Xavier in the Cintas Center in Cincinnati, Ohio. From the field he took 12 shots and made 12, from the three-point range he made three, and then from the free throw line he took six shots and made all six. As fans from both sides realized what was happening, there was more interest in whether Delonte could keep it going than in the game score. Many breathless oohs and aahs came from the crowd until the game ended with an 81-73 victory for St. Joe's. For this incredible feat, Delonte was awarded Player of the Week honors from the Atlantic 10, the Big 5, and the *Sporting News*.

Pat Carroll was close but not quite perfect when he made seven out of nine shots and contributed 20 points in the Massachusetts contest. When the team met and defeated St. Bonaventure the last week in January to make it 17-0, they officially set the school record for the most consecutive wins. In this game, Pat missed only one of his attempts and added 17 to the win column. After the St. Bonaventure game, Pat was awarded Player of the Week by both the Atlantic 10 and Big 5.

A new radio show debuted at nearby Carmella's Restaurant to keep fans abreast on news and comments on the fabulous Saint Joseph's Hawks. Phil Martelli was a guest on ESPN's *SportsCenter* television show. Comcast developed an entertaining series for television called *Hanging with the Hawks*.

Pete had found a way to make it to every game except the one against California in the Pete Newell Challenge back in December. Now the Nelson contingent was growing with each game. True cousins and people who called themselves cousins wanted to be there for Jameer, wanted to see him play before his sensational college career ended. To find enough tickets not being used took a few small miracles and the combined efforts of Clare Ariano and Caitlin Ryan in the men's basketball office, ticket manager Ron Joyce and his staff members Helen Hennessy, Kathy MacDonald and Trish Ryan, and athletic director Don DiJulia and his staff members Ellen Ryan and Eileen Brown.

The seemingly impossible became possible in February as they handily beat nearby rivals Villanova University and LaSalle University. Their coach said, "The mental makeup of this team astonishes me. That's as raucous an atmosphere as I've ever been in but you could see the calm in their faces." So that more of their fans could be together to see the Villanova game, a large screen television was set up at the field house on Hawk Hill. The LaSalle game was played in the Palestra and aired nationally on television by ESPN. Fan interest was so high for the University of Dayton game that television and radio stations in both Pennsylvania and Ohio aired the game. Wins over University of Dayton, University of Rhode Island and Fordham University put the Hawks at the 23-0 mark and moved them up to No. 2 in the national polls.

Tyrone Barley, Jameer's fellow senior, joined him in setting a new mark of 91 victories over their four years when they downed Fordham. With this victory, the Hawks also clinched the Atlantic 10 East crown. Jameer said about his fellow senior: "I told Ty after the game that I wouldn't want to spend my four years with anyone else. He's helped me out so much over the years. Just facing him every day in practice has helped me so much. He gives tremendous effort all the time."

Delonte continued his excellent scoring to reach 1000 college career points in the game against LaSalle, and then he and Jameer were named to NABCs (National Association of Basketball Coaches) All-District Team. Jameer earned the Atlantic 10 Player of the Week for the seventh time.

Hawk Talk continued at Carmella's, and Phil appeared four more times on ESPN's *SportsCenter*. For the first time in the history of Saint Joseph's University, *Sports Illustrated* dedicated a cover to them. In the February 16 edition, Jameer appeared bigger than life on a grand cover back grounded in Saint Joseph's red with this caption: "Meet Jameer Nelson the little man from the little school that's beating everyone."

The inside story covered not only Jameer's success but also that of the team and the university. From the president of the university, Reverend

Pete with Father Lannon at the
2004 NCAA tournament.

Timothy Lannon, S.J., came these words: "We celebrate for Jameer Nelson, the men's basketball team and the entire university. This and all the national coverage we are receiving is a tribute to the coaches, student-athletes and staff who have worked so hard to make this such a special time on campus. The mission of Saint Joseph's University is one of excellence and of striving for more. We are blessed that our men's basketball program continues to represent that mission so positively to the nation."

The cover was so picture-perfect and appealing that Pete went out and bought as many copies as he could find and mounted them on red posters for friends and family to have as keepsakes.

There is a phenomenon known as the *Sports Illustrated* "cover jinx." This started with Volume 1, Issue 1, when major league baseball player Eddie Mathews was featured on the cover and then injured his hand, forcing him to miss seven games. Since then, a number of major mistakes, injuries and even deaths have occurred soon after athletes appeared on the cover. On the other hand, *Sports Illustrated* points out that Michael Jordan was on the cover 49 times and the New York Yankees 61 times with no apparent mishaps. Observers closely watched in the days and weeks after Jameer was on the cover to see what might befall him, but he and his team kept winning and getting awards.

Wins over Temple and then Massachusetts moved them to 25 wins with no losses. The Temple win gave them their second straight Philadelphia Big Five title. Both homemade and professional signs began appearing all over Philadelphia and its surrounding towns announcing 25-0, then 26-0 and finally 27-0 as they completed their season. The only other team that had a perfect record was Stanford University in California. Because the Pacific 10 conference in which Stanford played was considered stronger

Jameer cuts down the net after beating St. Bonnie's, 82-50, on March 2, 2004, making it a perfect 27-0 season. (AP/WWP)

than the Atlantic 10 conference, Stanford was ranked No. 1 and Saint Joseph's No. 2.

New slogans seemed to pop up every day. Headlines, posters and t-shirts were printed with "Jameeracle" and "Jameeracle on 54th Street". From wrestling came the term "Full Nelson," and the campus newspaper printed a story headlined with "A Jamerican Legend #14." Head coach Phil Martelli said he knew this was a "once in a lifetime" experience. Copies of Jameer's No. 14 jersey were made in all sizes and sold out in minutes. Little babies, lots of boys and girls and grownups had No. 14 on their front or back. One jersey with Jameer's autograph fetched $2,000 at a Catholic school's charity auction.

Although it was impossible to get a ticket for the games being held at Hawk Hill, the more popular name for Saint Joseph's Memorial Field House where the seating capacity was only 3,500, fans from every walk of life and from distant cities filled the much larger gyms at away games as they became aware that seeing Jameer play in college was becoming a once-in-a-lifetime possibility. Thousands of fans from the Philadelphia area traveled to Rhode Island, many of them driving over six hours through five states, to see the game. Although they had defeated Rhode Island earlier in the season by a good margin, this round was harder. They were within a minute of losing when

DIDJA HEAR 'BOUT JAMEER?

IT CAME AS NO GREAT surprise to Saint Joseph's coach Phil Martelli that Jameer Nelson would someday have his uniform retired and hanging from the walls of Alumni Fieldhouse. He knew the kid was special the first time he saw him play as a junior at Chester High.

It took the rest of us a little longer to realize just how special this 5-11 point guard was. Nelson was a deserving choice as National Player of the Year. He won every major award last season. Along the way, he helped resurrect the image of his hometown Chester, Pennsylvania and lift Saint Joseph's, the tiny Jesuit college in West Philadelphia, into the national spotlight, leading the Hawks to the No. 1 ranking at one point and a spot in the NCAA Regional finals.

And the best part, he never changed his principles or his personality. Jameer could have followed in the footsteps of so many other college stars, leaving school early for the NBA. Instead, he returned for his sen-

ior year to complete his education and, along with the late Guy Rodgers of Temple, became the standard for point guards in this basketball-rich city.

He is living proof that the Hawk will never die.

—Dick Weiss,
New York Daily Times

The stands were packed to capacity with fans wanting to be part of the spectacular 2003-2004 season for Jameer and St. Joe's. (Rick Stewart/Getty Images)

Delonte put up one of his precise three-pointers at the 57-second mark to give St. Joe's 57 points and the win.

As Saint Joseph's prepared for senior night, a night to honor Tyrone Barley, Robert Hartshorn, Brian Jesiolowski and Jameer, and the last home game of the season against St. Bonaventure's, new levels of security had to be put in place. A security clearance desk was set up to screen athletes from other sports coming and going from the gym on Hawk Hill. A few enterprising students walked into the field house with gym clothes and lacrosse sticks hoping to slide through. They were turned away with a smile and a "So sorry, good try."

Bodyguards were needed to assure his safety, as the number of fans wanting to be near, to speak to or get an autograph from Jameer grew into a large, pressing crowd. For the number of fans willing to stand in the cold to be near the game, the university put up a large screen just outside the field house to broadcast the game going on inside.

Their regular season became the perfect season with the final win against St. Bonnie's in early March. In 1991, Nevada-Las Vegas entered the NCAA tournaments undefeated. In the intervening 13 years, no other team had accomplished a perfect record. And now in 2004, it was not one of the powerhouse teams, but little St. Joe's that performed this remarkable feat. There was talk of retiring Jameer's No. 14 that night, but he said no, there were more games to be played.

Friends and families of the four graduating seniors were treated to a pregame dinner and were able to watch the game on a large-screen television on the comfortable chairs and sofas in Saint Joseph's Athletic Hall of Fame. Jameer's son had a grand time telling everyone that was his daddy on the television and playing with the other little children who had been invited. As the excitement grew, Jameer's mother, Linda, moved to the stands and was caught by the cameras doing great moves from her cheerleading days. When the game ended, everyone left the quiet and roominess of the Hall of Fame to descend on to the floor with the rest of the jubilant fans. Phil and the seniors gave marvelous speeches, and then all the coaches and players melted into the crowd to shake hands and hug. Pete pulled Elaine through the crowd so that the two of them could catch still another hug from Jameer on this most memorable night.

For basketball fans, March signals the start of what has become known as March Madness...the conference playoffs, the NCAA and NIT tournaments. For Saint Joseph's, the month began as March Magic. Jameer was named Player of the Year by ESPN.com and was profiled on ESPN's *Outside the Lines* television show. The team finally moved into the No. 1 ranking when Stanford was

*Jameer accepts the Atlantic 10 Conference Player
of the Year award from commissioner Linda
Bruno during the conference banquet on
March 9, 2004. (AP/WWP)*

defeated by Washington and received many honors at the Atlantic 10 Basketball Awards dinner.

Some thought the Hawks would breeze through the Atlantic 10 Conference playoffs but the Xavier squad had other ideas. Although they were defeated 81-73 by St. Joe's back in January, they had steadily improved throughout the season, and their head coach Thad Matta told them they would be playing the best team in college basketball. They took note, did their homework and were ready to take on the No. 1 team in the country. Xavier had a great start, played excellent defense and then executed a 71.1 shooting percentage in the Atlantic 10 quarter playoffs to bring down St. Joe's by a score of 87-67.

The 20-point loss was devastating after such a spectacular season. Those who thought Saint Joseph's did not deserve their No. 1 ranking because they were not part of a strong conference, and those who thought they were overrated took this loss as confirmation of their opinion. Coach Martelli, known to be a realist, simply said they lost to what was a better team that day. Jameer said: "We went down fighting. We didn't go down scared. It's going to make us hungrier."

For days after, the big question loomed: Would they lose their No. 1 seed as the NCAA Tournament approached?

Brian Jesiolowski (left), Jameer (center), and John Bryant (right) celebrate after being selected as a No. 1 seed in the 2004 NCAA tournament. (AP/WWP)

On Sunday, March 15, the news came and it was good. Saint Joseph's would be ranked No. 1 in the Eastern Regional. As they practiced and prepared to meet their first opponent in Liberty, the awards continued. Phil was named Coach of the Year and Jameer was named Player of the Year by the USBWA (United States Basketball Writers Association).

In the NCAA Eastern Regional, the Hawks first traveled to Buffalo, New York, to meet

Liberty University, a small college in Lynchburg, Virginia, that was easily defeated 82-63. Next came Bobby Knight and his Texas Tech that was tougher, but St. Joe's beat them, 70-65. These victories meant the next stop would be the Meadowlands in East Rutherford, New Jersey, to meet Wake Forest for the regional semifinal known as the Sweet Sixteen. Again, St. Joe's prevailed 84-80.

Onto the Elite Eight, where their next opponent was Oklahoma State.

With just seven seconds to go, the score was 62-61 in favor of St. Joe's, and it looked like the magic would continue for little St. Joe's as they would move on to the Final Four in San Antonio. Oklahoma State's John Lucas, whose father was an NBA player, sank a spectacular three-pointer from the left wing at 6.9 seconds moving the score to 64-62. The Hawks still had one possession left and issued the ball to Jameer who took a shot he had made many times before. It was a jumper from the lane, but the ball fell just short of the basket. Incredibly, their Cinderella story ended in a split second. Jameer dropped to the floor...an almost unbelievable ending to his college career.

As sad as this defeat was, the coach and players were enormously gracious. Phil said about Jameer: "I don't think you can put into words what this guy has done. He is the greatest player

Jameer sits on the floor after the loss to Oklahoma State. (AP/WWP)

I've ever been around. He is absolutely the nicest person anyone could ever imagine or want to be a part of their life. He's gone in terms of a uniform, but he'll never be gone from St. Joe's basketball. The numbers are astounding, and the wins are astounding, but the humanness with which he did it will last a lifetime in Saint Joseph's basketball history."

Jameer and coach Phil Martelli hug during a press conference after losing to Oklahoma State. (AP/WWP)

From Pat Carroll: "This was a magical season, and it's something we're going to take with us for the rest of our lives." From Tyrone Barley: "I'm so proud of my teammates that I'm not even dwelling on the negatives right now, even though this was my last game. That I've had the opportunity to play with the guys on my team, that's what I'm most pleased with." And Jameer echoed this with, "For me, it's about leaving my coaches and my teammates. It's not about the kind of season we had."

Jameer receiving the Bob Cousy Collegiate Point Guard of the Year Award from Bob Cousy at the Hall of Fame induction ceremony April 5, 2004 in San Antonio, Texas. (AP/WWP)

But recognition of what he and his team achieved did not end. Award after award came flowing in. Jameer was named Naismith Player of the Year and Phil was named Coach of the Year in honor of basketball's founder. These were awarded by Atlanta's Tip-off Club. Jameer was also the first recipient for the newly established Bob Cousy Point Guard Award and winner of the Oscar Robertson Trophy, named in honor of former NBA stars.

Phil was named Coach of the Year by the USBWA (United States Basketball Writers Association) as well as the Atlantic 10. Next came Jameer's unanimous selection to the *Associated Press* All-America Team. Then both player and coach received the Adolph Rupp Award by the Commonwealth of Kentucky for being the best in NCAA Division I basketball.

Jameer was named as one of the five finalists for the John Wooden Award and received the Senior Class Award as the best senior player. Player of the Year honors were issued by the Atlantic 10, NABC (National Association of Basketball Coaches), *Sports Illustrated*, ESPN.com, *Foxsports*, *Sporting News* and *Basketball Times*.

The Chevrolet Awards for the Best Player and Best Coach of the Year were presented in San Antonio during the Final Four games to Jameer and Phil on national television. In between the games, it was also announced that Jameer would be the recipient of the Bayer Senior CLASS Award to be awarded at the Overland Park Convention Center in Kansas in May. Dick Enberg of CBS Sports initiated this award in response to the growing trend for players to leave college early. The CLASS in the award is an acronym for Celebrating Loyalty and Achievement for Staying in School.

On April 19, Jameer was given a Day of Recognition by his hometown in Chester, Pennsylvania. He shared this special day with Kevin Jones, a Cardinal O'Hara graduate and All-America football player at Virginia Tech who was drafted in the National Football League by the Detroit Lions shortly after. In a student and invitations-only morning ceremony at Chester High School, Jameer's No. 14 jersey was retired. Then after a luncheon at City Hall, the public was invited to another celebration at the school district's athletic field. On Mother's Day, the Chester Elks sponsored a parade in Jameer and Kevin Jones's honor. For both occasions, Jameer and his family traveled in stretch limousines and were treated royally.

Four days later, Saint Joseph's filled their field house with as many tables and chairs as they could fit for a grand dinner and ceremony to retire Jameer's No. 14 jersey. As the evening came to an

Jameer and coach Phil Martelli sit beside their trophies after they were named Player and Coach of the Year by the Associated Press on April 2, 2004. (AP/WWP)

end, Jameer paid a special tribute to his father for all that he had done for him and pulled him close. They were both overcome with emotion and tears. Pete had been a Marine and maintains a decorum fitting of a Marine, but not that night. For several days after, his co-workers would good-naturedly smile and pretend to be sniffling whenever they crossed paths. But Pete did not mind. He knew they were happy for him and that all of them would love to have been in his shoes.

Early the next week it was time for more awards from the Philadelphia Big Five at the Herb

Good Club dinner. Saint Joseph's was named Team of the Year. Phil received the honor of Coach of the Year and Jameer was the Player of the Year. Phil was given the Harry Litwack Award as Philadelphia's top coach, and Jameer was given the Robert V. Greasy Award as the city's Most Valuable Player. For the fourth time, he earned All-Big 5 First-Team honors. For the second time, he won the Guy Rodgers Award as the top point guard. The evening's events also included All-Big 5 First Team honors and the Cy Kasselman Award for free-throw accuracy for Delonte and All-Big 5 Second-Team honors for Pat.

The grandest award in collegiate basketball, comparable to the Heisman in football, is the John Wooden Award, named in honor of the legendary coach whose UCLA team won ten NCAA championships. This was to be given by the 93-year-old John Wooden himself at a black-tie dinner in Los Angeles, California. Pete watched the televised event from his home in Chester. He was not used to seeing his son in a tux, but there he was with the five finalists on national television that Saturday evening. As Jameer's name was announced as the winner, he felt almost as if he were right there with him, his pride enormous. His mind raced back to all the days they spent together getting ready for and going to games. How could all of that lead to this moment?

Jameer poses with legendary coach John Wooden after he won the John R. Wooden Award on April 10, 2004. (AP/WWP)

Jameer sat and chatted with John Wooden and then put his arm around him as if they were good old friends. He said: "All the trophies mean a lot to me, but sitting next to Coach Wooden means more to me than anything else. It's unbelievable. I can't express in words how much it means to receive an award with this man's name on it."

From Rob Knox, sportswriter for the Delaware County *Daily Times*, came these words: "Instead of being on the floor with any number of NBA stars this past season, Nelson was the leader of a special team, which landed him on a distinguished and permanent list featuring some of the greatest college basketball players in history. You know the names: Larry Bird, Ralph Sampson, Michael Jordan, Phil Ford, David Robinson, Chris Mullin, Danny Manning, Sean Elliot, Lionel Simmons, Christian Laettner, Glenn Robinson, Tim Duncan. Nelson joined that elite fraternity when he completed a rare sweep of every major Player of the Year Award when he was bestowed the John Wooden Award."

When Jameer was young, there were those who said he could never make it in basketball because of his height. In a wonderful turn of events, his 2004 sweep of awards would not have been a clean sweep if he had been one of those tall players. At the Basketball Hall of Fame in Springfield, Massachusetts, he received the Frances Pomeroy Naismith Award for being the best senior player under six feet.

CHAPTER 8

The Pride of Chester, St. Joe's, and Philadelphia

The city of Chester, Pennsylvania, is located about 15 miles south of Philadelphia. Its history goes back to William Penn, who in 1682 landed where Chester is now located and whose name Penn's Woods was transformed into Pennsylvania. By the late 1800s, it was a thriving city, and in the early 1900s, it became known for its industry and economic growth. After the second World War, however, the city was hit hard as the U.S. economy moved from manufacturing to services. Many of its manufacturing industries closed or moved to other locations, and both the number of jobs and the population dropped by about one-third.

When you drive into the city, what you notice most are the streets of row houses, most of them red brick with a front porch, a patch of green in the front and a backyard. They are not large or luxurious but comfortable and practical, typically with a living room, dining room and kitchen on the first floor and then three bedrooms and a bath on the second floor.

Interspersed are many small, independent businesses to serve the community—barbershops, food take-outs, laundries, small grocery stores, bars and jazz clubs. There are many churches, some of them large and sturdy, others smaller and located in what used to be a store or office building. And there are athletic fields and facilities where there is a lot of action and tremendous support from many of the people who live nearby.

The families that elected to stay in Chester are often very committed to their community. There is a lot of warmth, a lot of compassion here and opportunity to be great again. Many remember when it was a safe and cordial community, when people would stop to give you a lift in their cars to save you bus money, when you could leave a $20 bill on the counter, walk away and know it would be there when you got back.

Widener University elected to stay in Chester and is involved in its redevelopment. Surrounding the campus are restaurants, bed and breakfast homes and hotels. Nearby is the Crozer-Chester Medical Center whose parent company, Crozer

Keystone Health Systems, is the largest employer in Delaware County. Recently, Synergy elected to locate its headquarters in Chester along the Delaware as part of the Wharf at Rivertown, a redevelopment effort for the old historic power plant that will include parks, picnic areas, fishing piers and a marina in addition to office buildings, stores and restaurants.

Groups of concerned citizens took note that as the economy of Chester spiraled down, it had become a target location for companies involved in trash and infectious waste. Studies and legislative movements were started to stop this dangerous trend and have met with success.

Throughout the years, two important parts of Chester remained committed and these were its school system and its proud, rich tradition of Chester High basketball. From Alonzo Lewis, Chester's coach prior to Fred Pickett: "The thing you have to understand about Chester is the mentality of the fans. They expect to win and be in the state finals, nothing less. There is more pressure from them than from anywhere else. They're critical, and they'll tell you how they think you're doing."

Those who have been involved in the school system and community feel that Jameer Nelson's story will have an immediate and major impact on the kids. There is hope that it will shed a different light to outsiders on what the city of Chester is all about.

Jameer has shown that a strong will, hard work and determination to be the best you can be can make a difference. It will open the door for those who have a desire to be somebody, to do something important. Along the way, he has taken time to show how much he has appreciated the people who were there for him throughout the years...his family, his friends, his educators and coaches.

When he was a student and player at Chester High School, he was encouraged to talk to reporters, to be interviewed and to be prepared to meet the public. He is particularly comfortable with kids and will likely continue to be a spokesman for them as he moves into his professional career.

For Saint Joseph's University, the impact of Jameer, Coach Martelli and the 2003-2004 basketball team will be felt for many years to come. Their win count, the first No. 1 ranking, and new individual records were the best in the 95-year history of the program. When it came to athletic records and awards, the sheer number of them may never be beaten. Although there were very high hopes at the start of the season, no one could have predicted all that came to be.

At first it was mostly those at the university and in and around Philadelphia who were rooting for Saint Joseph's, but as they marched toward a perfect season and then into the Elite Eight of the NCAA Tournament, people all across the country took notice and began rooting for "little St. Joe's." It was a Cinderella story that was highlighted by the fracas from basketball analyst Billy Packer's comments on whether Saint Joseph's deserved to be rated No. 1. The controversy and comments that ensued caught the attention of the media and the fans and pitted the little guy against the big powerhouses in collegiate basketball.

When the team traveled to other parts of the United States to play in the NCAA tournament, they were recognized and surrounded at airports and hotels. Hundreds of kids waited outside for a chance to see them when they were practicing at a gym.

USA Today had a front-page story titled "$2 million—A Star Player's Value" that focused on the many ways Jameer's success would be generating revenue for Saint Joseph's. Some could not be precisely measured: the upsurge in applications to attend the university, the interest in athletes to join Saint Joseph's programs, the national recognition, savings on marketing and recruiting costs. Others had a definite economic value, such as their athletic merchandising of clothing, programs, and other items, their ticket sales to games, their share of proceeds from tournament games, new scheduling and television possibilities. Some analysts guesstimated the value now and over the next few years at $1 million, others said it might be high as $2 million. Looking at this in cold, hard numbers, the investment of about $130,000 in scholarships for Jameer over his four years at the school had incredible returns.

For Jameer and many of the others closely involved in the program, money was not and will not be the issue. His desire to have a college education, to continue to play his favorite sport, to have fun and enjoy the camaraderie he had with his teammates and coaches, to build his skills and be recognized by many others for all of his hard work, to have made his family very proud...these were the things that were really important.

On the top of six skyscrapers in downtown Philadelphia were lights patterned to display this gigantic message: CONGRATS ST. JOE'S YOU'VE MADE PHILLY PROUD. Both Jameer and Phil were given keys to the City of Philadelphia by Mayor John Street and were honored with a special day at a Phillies game where Phil got to throw the first ball and Jameer sat in the dugout with Larry Bowa and the rest of team, wearing a baseball shirt with his No. 14 emblazoned on it. In addition to Phil's regular radio show, the Philadelphia television stations frequently featured the Hawks, had their players, coaches and others associated with the basketball program on as guest stars. As the season mounted success after success, the *Philadelphia Inquirer* and *Daily News* featured many full-color photos to spread the news.

Near the end of June, Saint Joseph's men's basketball team received the prestigious 2004 John Wanamaker Award as "the athlete, team or organization that has done the most to reflect credit upon Philadelphia and the team or sport in which they excel." The Philadelphia Sports Congress, IPC/Amerimar Management, CBS-TV and the Philadelphia *Daily News* joined forces to present the award ceremony and luncheon.

Saint Joseph's season was hailed as the Cinderella, Hoosiers and Sea Biscuit stories all rolled into one. Philadelphia is a tremendous sports town, and its ups and downs frequently follow those of its sports teams. Many were uplifted to hear that Jim O'Brien, who had played basketball with great success at Saint Joseph's, would be back in town as the new head coach of the 76ers. Back in the fall, the Eagles made it to the National Football League conference championships. Then early in May, a Philadelphia horse named Smarty Jones won the Kentucky Derby and two weeks later the Preakness. He is one of a handful of horses who had remained undefeated while also winning horse racing's major events. The Philadelphia Flyers skated their way to the Eastern Conference finals of the National Hockey League. All in all it was a very good year for those in Philadelphia who love sports and love to win.

Although Jameer is firm in saying he will always be from Chester, Pennsylvania, the big city nearby hopes that he will add that it was in the city of Philadelphia where he went to college, led his team to a perfect season and then became the most celebrated basketball player of all time in a single season.

CHAPTER 9

What's Next?

Soon after the NCAA tournament ended, Jameer signed an agreement to have Steve Mountain of Cornerstone Management as his agent. In addition to all the award banquets, he made special appearances at a number of locations in the Philadelphia area. As the 2004 NBA draft neared, he had to pull away and begin to prepare.

This put him back in his favorite place...the basketball court, working out daily, sometimes with his Saint Joseph's teammates, sometimes with his good friend Doug Overton who had over ten years of professional basketball experience, most recently with the Los Angeles Clippers. Jameer also visited with a number of the NBA teams and made a public relations appearance at the predraft camp in Chicago.

Pete with son Maurice and grandson Meer-meer.

As Jameer won trophy after trophy, Phil Martelli joked that he would need to build a bigger house to hold all of them. He has offered to do just that and build two houses when he has the funds, one for his mother and one for his father.

At this time, Pete thinks he will decline the offer and stay in Chester, continuing his work as a welder, continuing to be with Maurice at his baseball, basketball and football games and continuing to be close to his family and friends. Right now, Maurice and little Meer-meer physically wear each other out whenever they play together. In the not too distant future, Meer-meer may begin playing organized sports. And whenever he can, Pete will be right there with his grandson as he has been for his sons.

Like Jameer, coach Phil Martelli also won an incredible number of awards in the spring of 2004. He has said this past year was a "once in a lifetime" occurrence, but he will be trying for more winning seasons for Saint Joseph's University. He balances his time between preparing for the future and spending time with those who want to honor him for what he has accomplished to date.

Just before the start of each basketball season, there is a special night called Hawks Hoops Hysteria at the field house. It is similar to the Midnight Madness held at many colleges and universities where the students are invited for a fun evening of food, festivities, an introduction to this year's team and then a game that goes on into the wee hours of the morning. Phil Martelli added to St. Joe's unique version a return of all the previous players, managers and coaches they can round up, sometimes going back as many as seven decades. Before the intra-squad scrimmage with this year's players, an alumni reception and game is held. Phil, along with Jameer's teammates and many others will be hoping in the years to come that

Jameer can break away from his professional schedule to come back and spend another night with them.

Around the basketball courts in the city of Chester, stories about Jameer and his moves will be added to those of the legends before him: Emerson Baynard, Granville "Granny" Lash, Horace Walker, Mike Marshall, Billy and Jerry Foster. Many remember the day back in the 1960s when Lew Alcindor and several of his buddies traveled all the way from New York to find top action at "The Cage" in Chester, a set of two courts surrounded by a high fence that attracted the best players around. Word spread from door to door, from telephone to telephone, and soon just about everyone came out to see what one young boy named Randy Legette described as "the tallest jokers in the whole world" and "the best that New York City had to offer." Jameer's dazzling play and accomplishments will no doubt be added to this rich tradition of Chester basketball.

In Jameer's professional contract, provision has been made to have the money manager secure tickets and make arrangements for his mother and father and Meer-meer to travel to as many of his NBA games as they can. He adores his son and looks forward most of all to being with him. As he has done in his college years, he will be opening up as much time as possible to be with him.

Jameer continued to drive his "old jalopy" but made plans to find a great-looking automobile. Instead of a little sporty car, he chose a Cadillac Escalade with plenty of space for extra passengers. He also continued to work toward wrapping up his final academic requirements for receiving his bachelor's degree in sociology from Saint Joseph's University.

Many of his fans hoped the team that selected Jameer would be the Philadelphia 76ers or the New Jersey Nets so that they could continue to see Jameer play in person. Others from his close circle thought it would be better to be on a team farther away, so that Jameer could have a little more space, a little more breathing room as he begins this next phase of his life. As draft day neared, there was much speculation as to just which team would be the one. On his visits across the country, no NBA team had told Jameer with certainty that he was their first choice.

For the NBA draft, Jameer was invited to sit in the Green Room, an area reserved for those players thought to be definite first-round picks and their chosen guests. Jameer invited his parents, Linda and Pete, his son Meer-meer, his mentor Earl Pearsall, his coach Phil Martelli, and his agent Steve Mountain. Seated in the stands in Madison Square Garden in New York was a cheering group of family and friends along with over 100 Saint Joseph's fans.

Jim O'Brien, the newly appointed head coach of the Philadelphia 76ers, had announced that his team would not be selecting Jameer, but some of his supporters secretly hoped this would change as deals and arrangements were made throughout the course of the draft. A number of basketball experts predicted Jameer would be selected anywhere from the seventh pick to the thirteenth. But these spots came and went and it was clear that this had become the year for the high-school players who had decided to skip college. The NBA was selecting on potential rather than experience, adding extra high-energy years to the young players' careers.

Although Linda and Pete continued to have faith, the cameras zoned in on Jameer as numbers fourteen, fifteen, sixteen, seventeen, eighteen and nineteen went by. Pete leaned over and said "Son, you're going to get picked. I don't know when, but you will be picked." Jameer said, "I know," then smiled at the cameras and put his head to his young son's and waited.

Finally ... at long last ... when number twenty was announced by NBA commissioner David Stern, Jameer was selected by the Denver Nuggets. He said, "Hey, Dad, I made it. I'll show everyone what I can do. I always get the job done." He

Jameer shakes hands with NBA commissioner David Stern after being drafted by the Denver Nuggets in the first round of the NBA Draft on June 24, 2004. (AP/WWP)

moved to the podium, put on the draft cap for the Nuggets and flashed his extraordinary smile. From ESPN's Dick Vitale, to Coach Martelli and many of those who had followed Jameer's extraordinary high school and college careers, the thought that prevailed was, "What was the NBA thinking?"

Within just a few minutes, everything changed. An announcement was made that the Nuggets traded Jameer to the Orlando Magic for a future first-round pick. John Weisbrod, Orlando's general manager, very much wanted

Jameer reacts during a news conference after he is traded to the Orlando Magic within minutes of being drafted by the Denver Nuggets. (AP/WWP)

DIDJA HEAR 'BOUT JAMEER?

MEER, A COACH'S DREAM; orchestrates, demands and brings out the best in his teammates. He simply wills his team to victory, with a stare, a pass, a rebound or a much-needed shot. All from the love and respect he has for the game we call basketball.

—Fred Pickett,
Head boys basketball coach,
Chester High School

Jameer but did not think he would still be available to them. Because there is a fixed pay scale that reduces with each selection pick, it was thought by many that Orlando landed the very best bargain in the entire NBA draft.

Two opposing camps developed in the basketball world. One believes that the NBA's increased recruiting of the best high school players will hurt many college programs, that a number of players who would benefit from a college education and experience will miss this opportunity, that there is too much emphasis on money. Others are equally strong in voicing their opinion that if players have the opportunity to earn millions of dollars, they should grab it while they can.

To Jameer, this was just another challenge he would take head on. He thought it was a blessing in disguise, that he would be very much wanted and needed by the Magic in the rebuilding of their team, that there were great players and very good people involved in this organization. That he was passed over by nineteen teams has created what he calls "a chip on his shoulder" that he will use to prove that he can get the job done and done very well.

Although he would have liked to have continued his career in the Philadelphia area to have more time with his son, Orlando is just a two-hour plane ride away. One of his first purchases

Jameer looks to pass during an NBA summer league game at Cox Pavilion in Las Vegas on July 14, 2004. (AP/WWP)

DIDJA HEAR 'BOUT JAMEER?

JAMEER AND I WENT to Toby Farms Elementary together and then I moved to Atlanta for a few years. When I came back to Pennsylvania, I was fifteen years old. I lived with Pete and his family. At first, Jameer and I fussed and fought like brother and sister, usually about petty stuff.

Then when we went to Chester High, we got along much better. Every year there, we had at least one class together. I had taken French since sixth grade, so I was able to help him with this. We worked together to get through many classes. In 10th, 11th and 12th grade, we were very close and basically laughed our way through high school. I had always wanted to have a Mazda Millennia and we would joke about this.

The possibility of making it to the NBA was so far-fetched when we were in high school. Jameer was never arrogant or self-centered, he did not brag or say he would make it to NBA. But I always knew he was good enough to make it. The NBA is a one-in-a-million shot, and I guess Jameer is that one.

No matter what happens, I am very proud of Jameer's accomplishments, always have and always will be. He has not only made a great name for himself and his family, but he has also made people see Chester in a whole different light. The same light we've been trying to shine for years.

Best of luck, Jameer.

—Tyona Burton,
cousin

with his new NBA salary was a modest home in the Orlando area so that he could have Meer-meer and his family and friends for extended visits. And with Disney World nearby, for a few hours here and there, everyone can be just a kid having fun.

Jameer has signed a shoe contract with Converse. In the near future, there will be Jameer Nelson sneakers right along with the renowned Chuck Taylors. When he returned home to Chester for vacation, Jameer came loaded with shorts, jerseys and shoes for his younger brother Maurice. One was a light blue Magic jersey with Jameer's No. 14. Maurice put it on and flew right out the door to show the other kids in the neighborhood.

Although many who have grown up in the cities and towns surrounding Philadelphia and then moved to another part of the world go on to say they are "from Philadelphia," Jameer has resolutely stated that he will never forget Chester and will "always be from Chester, Pennsylvania."

Floyd "Pete" Nelson

Floyd "Pete" Nelson was born in Wilmington, North Carolina. His parents Doris and Nathaniel moved to Philadelphia, Pennsylvania, when he was five and here he lived through his school years until he joined the Marines.

The family included six sons, no daughters. Their names were Anthony, Duvall ("Duke"), Floyd ("Pete"), James, Johnny and Lloyd. James, Pete and Duke were a threesome, being close in age, who hung out together and played sports together. They could often be seen shooting baskets at Fitzsimmons Junior High.

Very few of his many friends have known him as Floyd. When he was very little, his grandmother called him "Peaches," and this nickname stuck.

But as he grew up and ventured onto the streets of Philadelphia, there was no way he could continue to be called "Peaches" so this was transformed into "Pete," and became the name by which he is known to most.

When his school days were done, he decided he wanted to get away from home and see more of the world, so he signed up to be a Marine, was accepted and then surprised his parents with the news. In the 1970s during the Vietnam War, he served in the ground forces and was shot in the line of duty.

When his tour was completed, he returned to the Philadelphia area to find a job and landed one as a welder with British Petroleum to construct ships in Chester, just south of Philadelphia along the Delaware River. He continued with BP for 23 years and then with Hayes Tug and Launch, where the ships he helped to build included the *Liberty Bell III* at Penn's Landing in Philadelphia.

His marriage to Linda produced three sons: Floyd "Pete" Jr., Jabre who died as an infant, and Jameer. When Jameer was very young, he and Linda divorced. Both remarried, she to John Billings and he to Elsie Plummer. A fourth son, Maurice, was born 10 years after Jameer.

Although Jameer officially lived with Linda until he was 12 and then with Pete the next 10 years, he had easy access to both parents as they continued to be friends and lived near to each other in Chester. Pete became the guiding force, the chauffeur and arranger for his sons' participation in sports. Not only did a love of sports transfer to his sons, but also much of his genial personality, his strong moral character and his love for people.

In addition to his presence at his sons' games, Pete also became known for his barbeques. His father-in-law James Holland first taught him how to do it right from the building of a pit to preparation of the meat to putting together the ingredients needed for a great sauce. Pete went on to develop a special sauce of his own and would cook not only at his home in Chester but also on the road for Jameer's teammates as they traveled around the country playing ball.

One of the many community services he has performed has been to be a regular blood donor. He is particularly proud of a pin he received when he reached the five-gallon mark and is continuing on to another five gallons.

Pete leads a very busy life. In addition to his weekday work as a welder, he conducts welding seminars on weekends. Then with all of the activities of his family and his many friendships, he keeps hopping. He hopes to gather more stories to tell as he continues to play an active role in his youngest son Maurice's sports and someday those of his grandson, Jameer Jr.

In addition to Meer-meer, he is called "Pop-pop Pete" by six other grandchildren: Tamara's daughter Jucae and son Jaqual, Pete Jr.'s daughters Grecia and Janise, and Althea's daughter Brianna and son Anthony.

Elaine Whelan

A joke in the Whelan household has been that Elaine must have signed a marriage contract agreeing to attend 5,000 basketball games for every play or concert attended by her husband Charles (also known as "Chuck").

It was at a basketball game at Chester High School, where Charles and his friend Mike Galante were looking for players for their Donofrio team, that she first met Jameer Nelson. Like them, she thought he was someone very special.

Elaine first saw her husband and his twin brother Gene play basketball when their high school Haverford was in competition with her high school Abington for the Suburban District I championship. She did not actually meet him

until five years later when both were working at
Sun Oil Company in Philadelphia.

Charles had just completed his tour of duty
with the Strategic Air Command, where he and
Gene had played on the Air Force touring team
and scrimmaged with the professional Cincinnati
Royals. The twins next won full scholarships to
play Division I basketball at Loyola College in

Maryland. Then, before sophomore year, Elaine and Chuck married and both became part of the basketball crowd at Loyola. They were also friends with Tommy Hawkins, Wayne Embry, Jerry Lucas and others from the Royals and whenever they were playing in Baltimore, would get together.

When their son, Chad, reached his teenage years and became a star player at Chestnut Hill Academy and then Souderton High School, they decided to sponsor a team in the Donofrio Classic postseason tournament for high school students.

Through this and other sponsorships, they came to know many of the best high school players in the Philadelphia area, and college coaches often looked to Charles to help find outstanding players. In turn, some of the boys who needed a helping hand, a caring adult, were given this.

It was her writing skills that first attracted the attention of her teachers and counselors at Abington High School and motivated them to help her win a full scholarship to Drexel University, where she went on to graduate with first honors. She next studied philology, the history of languages, at the University of Pennsylvania while she worked in research at Sun Oil Company and then Towers, Perrin, Forster and Crosby.

After her marriage to Charles Whelan, she moved to Baltimore and was recruited by the Social Security Administration, where she received extensive computer education provided by IBM Corporation. While there, the federal government sponsored her graduate studies in advanced statistics for research at Johns Hopkins University. She participated in a number of pioneering projects and concluded her time with SSA on the Commissioner's staff focused on the projects to assign Social Security numbers to newborns and to provide part-time professions to women with children.

Soon after the Whelan's return to Pennsylvania when Charles was assigned a sales engineer's territory with Armco Steel, their son Chad was born. Elaine next sold the concept of having a part-time professional to Krall Management Incorporated, where she worked a three-day schedule as a systems consultant for five years until the birth of their second child, Christie.

When she returned to work, she met her first partner, Myles Strohl, and together they founded Strohl Systems. It was here that the DentaLab system that became the focus of the landmark U.S. Supreme Court case *Whelan v. Jaslow* was first developed. This case confirmed the use of the copyright laws for protection of computer software and defined the scope of this protection. In 2003, this case became the subject of Elaine's book, *My Mom's Making History—The Story of*

Computer Software, Copyrights and Creativity, directed toward teaching the history and purpose of copyrights to students. This book is now required reading in many schools.

The participants in this book developed the Copyrights Promote Creativity Project. Through this, she became involved with the Pennsylvania State University's programs involving copyright conferences and workshops for educators. In the next school year, she will, along with Penn State's Dr. Matt Jackson, be the guest speaker at a number of colleges and universities involved in copyright education.

In conjunction with her work as president of Mainstreet Systems & Software where the DentaLab systems have continued to be developed, Elaine has been a regular columnist for three journals of dental technology in the United States and Canada. In 2001, she was cited by the *Journal of Dental Technology* as a visionary in the field of software for dentistry.

Since her first book on her own story, Elaine has been asked to write or help write the stories of others. She hopes to continue to do this and make it her part-time vocation when someday she retires or semi-retires from her work with computer systems.

She and her husband live on a white pine farm in a rural village near Philadelphia, where they raise Bouvier des Flandres dogs and sponsor youth basketball. They are the parents of Chad and Christie and the grandparents of Bryn and Ruth.

For Additional Information:

If you would like further details from their archives, here are the websites for the basketball programs at:

Chester High School
www.eteamz.com/chesterclippers

Saint Joseph's University
www.sjuhawks.com

If you would like to contact the authors, send an email message through:

www.promotecopyrights.com
or
www.SportsPublishingLLC.com

Celebrate the Heroes of Pennsylvania Sports
and College Basketball in These Other 2004 Releases from Sports Publishing!

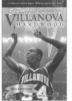